Human Nature

HUMAN NATURE

D.W. WINNICOTT

Schocken Books / New York / 1988

#1735467

First American Edition
Copyright © 1988 by The Winnicott Trust
By arrangement with Mark Paterson

Library of Congress Cataloging-in-Publication Data

Winnicott, D. W. (Donald Woods), 1896–1971.
  Human nature.

  Bibliography: p.
  Includes index.
  1. Child analysis. 2. Child psychology.
  3. Mind and body. I. Title
RJ504.2.W54 1988   618.92'89   87-43306
ISBN 0-8052-4046-2

Psychotherapy Book Club offers books and cassettes. For information
write: 230 Livingston St., Northvale, NJ 07647.

CONTENTS

PREFACE

by Clare Winnicott

In 1936 Donald Winnicott was invited by Susan Isaacs to lecture on Human Growth and Development to experienced teachers of young children on an advanced course in the University of London. In 1954 when this book was started he had also been lecturing regularly to University Social Work students since 1947. These opportunities for regular lecturing which continued until his death in 1971 were much valued by Winnicott because they provided him with a constant incentive to clarify his own understanding, and to modify his ideas in the light of his interaction with students, and of his own experience. It would be true to say that his lecturing activities were an integral part of his own development, and he felt deeply his gratitude to Susan Isaacs whose confidence in him was the first step to his participation.

Winnicott evolved his own special way of communicating the material of his lectures, and year after year students gave up trying to take notes, and became involved with him in the actual process of growth and development. In other words, they were learning without being taught. His lectures could be free and seem unstructured only because they were based on a central core of integrated knowledge and a carefully formulated pattern of the stages of human development which the students could comprehend. His rapidly constructed diagrams on the blackboard will be remembered by all who attended his lectures as an essential feature of his way of communicating.

The original purpose of this book was to supply the notes that the students could not take, and to make them available for all students of human nature. The first draft of the book was begun and completed in a comparatively short space of time in the summer of 1954, but ever since then until the time of his death it was under review and revision.

EDITORIAL NOTE

THE PLAN OF THE BOOK   *Winnicott made two synopses of his book on Human Nature. The first is dated August, 1954, which as we know from Clare Winnicott was when most of the book was written, and the second dates from around 1967. Both are reproduced in an Appendix at the end of the present volume.*

It can be seen that the material of the book follows the first three Parts of Synopsis I fairly closely even though the order of writing becomes somewhat different: for example, the proposed section on the "Study of Sequences" including fantasy, inner reality and dream, as well as that on "Transitional objects and phenomena" did not materialise according to the plan, most likely because these subjects had already been touched upon in previous chapters. It will also be seen from Synopsis I that Winnicott's original plan included two further Parts with chapters on the antisocial tendency and the various stages in development from latency to maturity which in fact were never written, though there is evidence that he was going to begin the next Part with a paper entitled "Delinquency Research" which had been published in 1943 in the journal New Era in Home and School.

The second synopsis may possibly have been intended as a guide to revision of the book. It is noticeable that Parts I and III of the book in its present form are summarised in this synopsis much as they actually occur, but it seems that Winnicott might have intended to curtail the present Part II (dealing with Interpersonal Relationships and Instinct Theory); and of the last eight chapters in the present Part IV only that on "Environment" is listed.

THE HEADINGS   *The headings of the separate Parts, Chapters and Sections that occur in the present volume are nearly all as they were found in the type-* script. *In the very few places where we have added a section heading for the sake of consistency we have consulted the synopses.*

THE TEXT   *This has been left as it was found. Corrections that were made to the typescript in Winnicott's writing or in that of Joyce Coles, his* secretary, *have been incorporated; but in the few places where we have added a word or letter these appear in square brackets. Any footnotes or parts of footnotes that we have added also appear in square brackets.*

NOTES FOR REVISION   *A number of notes in Winnicott's writing were found with the typescript showing where and how he wished to revise certain sections of the* book. *Most of these were on separate small pieces of paper giving the number of the page to which they referred; but very occasionally such notes were found written in the margin of the typescript. All of these notes now appear as footnotes to the text at the place where the revision was intended.*

Christopher Bollas
Madeleine Davis
Ray Shepherd

ACKNOWLEDGEMENT

We are grateful to have been able to use work on bibliographical details and on the index done by Judith Issroff.

INTRODUCTION

T HE TASK is the study of human nature.

At the moment of starting to write this book I am all too aware of the vastness of such an enterprise. Human nature is almost all we have.

In spite of knowing this I do intend to keep to the title, and I do intend to make a statement of human nature which gathers together the various types of experience which have been mine: what I have learned from my teachers and from my clinical experiences. In this way I may achieve a personal and therefore understandably limited description of a theme that is without limits.

It is really much easier, and more usual, for a doctor to write about illness. Through the study of illness we come to the study of much that is important about health. But the doctor's assumption that health is a relative absence of disease is not good enough. The word health has its own meaning in a positive way, so that absence of disease is no more than the starting point for healthy life.

I shall take as my reader the postgraduate student who can be relied on to have read a certain amount of psychology of the dynamic kind, and to have had personal experiences, both in work and in life and living.

The reader is entitled to know how it is that I come to be able to write about psychology. My professional life has been spent in paediatrics. Whereas my paediatric colleagues mostly specialised on the physical side I myself gradually veered round towards specialisation on the psychological side. I have never left general paediatrics, for it seems to me that child psychiatry is essentially part of paediatrics. Whereas adult psychiatry must unfortunately be split off from medical and surgical practice, this splitting off need never occur where infants and children are concerned.

Through having personal difficulties I came into psycho-analysis at an early stage of my work as a children's doctor. Soon I began to see that there was a place for the psycho-analysis of children, both as a therapy and as a research method. In 1927 I came into contact with Melanie Klein's application of Freud's methods to child therapy, and later I discovered that Aichhorn, Anna Freud and Alice Balint and others had in various ways started to apply psycho-analysis to childhood problems, and I had opportunity to learn from Anna Freud who came to settle in London.

I became a student at the Institute of Psycho-Analysis, and after qualification as an analyst and then as a child analyst I was able to undertake adult and child analyses in almost all types of case and from any age group. However, the experience of any one analyst must remain but that of one person. It is only possible for an analyst to carry through about seventy analyses. By the nature of my practice I was able to get round this difficulty of limitation of case-experience by having in my care a vast number of patients in my out-patient work, and by undertaking innumerable short psycho-therapies, and management problems.

I avoided the immensely exacting organised antisocial case during the early stages of my career, but in the war became forced to consider this type of disorder through the work I was privileged to do with evacuated children in Oxfordshire.

At about this time I was also gradually lured into the treatment of the more psychotic type of adult patient, and I found that I could learn much about the psychology of early infancy from adults deeply regressed in the course of psycho-analytic treatment, much of which could not be learned by direct observation of infants, nor from analysis even of children of 2 ½ years. This psycho-analytic work with adults of psychotic type proved extremely exacting and time-absorbing and by no means always obviously successful. In one case that ended tragically I gave 2500 hours of my professional life, without hope of remuneration. Nevertheless this work taught me more than any other one kind.

Binding all this together there has been the constant need to give advice to parents in consultation, and it is this giving of advice that I have found most difficult.

Lastly I mention the stimulus of teaching and broadcasting.

PART I

THE HUMAN CHILD EXAMINED:
SOMA, PSYCHE, MIND

INTRODUCTION

I HAVE CHOSEN to look at human nature through a study of the child. Although in health the adult continues to grow, develop and change right up to the moment of death, there is a pattern already to be discerned in the child which will persist, just as the face remains recognisable throughout the life of the individual.

But, where is the child to be found?

The child's body belongs to the paediatrician.
The soul belongs to the minister of religion.
The psyche belongs to the dynamic psychologist.
The intellect belongs to the psychologist.
The mind belongs to the philosopher.
Psychiatry claims mental disorder.
Heredity belongs to the geneticist.
Ecology claims an interest in the social milieu.
Social science studies the family setting and its relation to society as well as to the child.
Economics examines the strains and stresses due to conflicting needs.
The law steps in to regularise and humanise public revenge on account of antisocial behaviour.

In contrast with the multiplicity of these various claims the individual human animal provides a unit and a central theme, and it is necessary for us to try to gather together in one complex statement the comments that can be made from the many vantage points.

There is no need to adopt one method and one method alone for the description of human beings. Rather it is profitable to become familiar with the use of each and every known method of approach.

In choosing a developmental approach to the study of human nature as the one that can focus the various points of view, I shall hope to make clear [how] first from a primary merging of the individual with the environment comes an emergence, the individual staking a claim, becoming able to be in a world that is disclaimed; then the strengthening of the self as an entity, a continuity of being, as a place where, and where from the self as a unit, as something body-bound and dependent on physical care [emerges]; then the dawning awareness (and awareness implies the existence of mind) of dependence, and awareness of the mother's dependability and of her love, which comes through to the infant as physical care and close adaptation to need; then the personal acceptance of functions and of instincts with their climax, of the gradual recognition of mother as another human being, and along with this a change from ruthlessness to concern; then a recognition of the third party, and of love complicated by hate, and of emotional conflict; the whole of this being enriched by the imaginative elaboration of every function, and the growth of the psyche along with that of the body; also the specialisation of intellectual capacity, dependent on the quality of brain endowment; and again along with all this the gradual development of independence of environmental factors, leading eventually to socialisation.

It would be possible to start at the beginning and to work gradually forwards, but this would mean starting with the obscure and unknown and only later reaching to that which is common knowledge. This study of development will start with the child of 4 and will work backwards, reaching at long last the individual's beginning.

Let me say a word about physical health. Health of body implies physical functioning appropriate to the age of the child, and the absence of disease. The assessment and measurement of bodily health is a task that the paediatrician assumes, that is to say, bodily health in so far as body functioning is not disturbed by emotion, by emotional conflict, and by the avoidance of painful emotion.

From conception to puberty there is a steady and continuous

growth and development of function, and no one thinks of judging the physical development of a child except according to the child's age.

Assuming satisfactory child care there can be said to be a standard rate of development. Charts are always being worked out for measurement. We can use the data collected and sorted out, being ready, however, to allow for wide individual variations within the health concept.

Paediatrics was established chiefly on the study of physical diseases peculiar to childhood, with health as an absence of disease. Not long ago rickets was common, as well as many other disorders due to faulty feeding; pneumonia was a constant problem and frequently led to empyaema, now hardly ever seen in a London hospital; congenital syphilis was frequently diagnosed in a children's clinic and was not easy to treat; acute bone infections had to be dealt with by drastic surgical operation and painful after-care. But in thirty years the whole picture has changed.

A hundred years ago there was an even worse state of affairs, an almost complete muddle as to diagnosis and causation, and the first job of the older generation of paediatricians was the sorting out of disease entities. In those days there was not much time or place for the consideration of health as such, nor for the study of the difficulties that beset the physically healthy child through the fact of growing up in a society that is composed of human beings.

Now, because of the advance in diagnosis and treatment of bodily disorder, we find doctors who are fully equipped to deal with bodily ailments also looking at the ways in which body functioning is disturbed by such things as anxiety, and by faulty home management.*

A new generation of medical students is demanding instruction in

---

* I would like to mention Guthrie, author of *Functional Nervous Disorders in Childhood* (1907), not because he reached to great heights but because he was a pioneer to whom I owe the special climate at the Paddington Green Children's Hospital which made my appointment there in 1923 possible. After Guthrie's tragic death I was to carry on the work of his department, and I was not aware at the time that it was because of my own leanings towards the psychological in paediatrics that I was appointed to the consulting staff of the hospital.

psychology. Where shall they turn? Paediatric teachers themselves may have no understanding of psychology. There is in my opinion a real danger lest the more superficial aspects of child psychology be over-stressed. Either the external factor or heredity is blamed for everything. Psychiatric disease entities are collected and described in a clear-cut fashion that is false; tests of attainment or of personality are unduly reverenced; a child's happy appearance is too easily accepted as a sign of healthy emotional development.

What has the psycho-analyst to offer? He offers no easy solution, but instead he confronts the young paediatrician, already about thirty years old and a married man with a family, with a new subject at least as big as physiology. Moreover he says that to reach a position in child psychiatry comparable to his high standing in physical paediatrics the paediatrician must undergo a personal analysis as well as a special training.

This is hard, but there is no way round and there never will be. The paediatrician hesitates at such a hazard, and prefers to stick to physical paediatrics even if he must go far afield to find enough physical disease to cure and to prevent. But the time is coming when no further expansion of physical paediatrics will be needed in this country, and an increasing number of young paediatricians will be forced into child psychiatry. I long for this day, and have longed for it throughout three decades. But the danger is that the painful side of the new development will be avoided, and an attempt will be made to find a way round; theories will be reformulated, implying that psychiatric disorder is a product not of emotional conflict but of heredity, constitution, endocrine imbalance, and crude mismanagement. But the fact is that life itself is difficult, and psychology concerns itself with the inherent problems of individual development and of the socialisation process; moreover in childhood psychology we must meet the struggles that we ourselves have been through, though for the most part we have forgotten these struggles or have never been conscious of them.

CHAPTER I

THE PSYCHE–SOMA
AND THE MIND

A HUMAN BEING is a time-sample of human nature. The whole person is physical if viewed from one angle, psychological if viewed from another. There are the soma and the psyche. There is also a developing complexity of inter-relationship between the two, and an organisation of this relationship coming from that which we call the mind. Intellectual functioning, like the psyche, has as its somatic basis certain parts of the brain.

As watchers of human nature we can discern body, psyche and mental functioning.

We will not fall into the trap laid for us by the common usage of the terms "mental" and "physical". These terms are not descriptive of opposed phenomena. It is the soma and the psyche that are opposed. The mind is of an order special to itself, and must be considered as a special case of the functioning of the psyche–soma.*

It is necessary to note the fact that it is possible to look at human nature in the three ways indicated, and to study the causes of the division of interest. It will be especially interesting to enquire into the very early stages of psyche–soma dichotomy in the infant, and the beginnings of mental activity.

SOMATIC HEALTH   Bodily health implies good enough heredity and good enough nurture. The body in health is functioning at the correct age level. Accidents and environmental failures are being dealt with, so

---

* See Winnicott, D.W.: (1949) "Mind and its Relation to the Psyche–Soma".

that in time their ill-effect will be erased. Development goes on with the passage of time, and gradually the infant becomes the man or the woman, not too early, not too late. Middle age arrives in due course, with new appropriate changes, and eventually old age curbs the various functions till natural death follows as the final seal of health.

PSYCHE HEALTH   In a similar way, health of the psyche is to be assessed in terms of emotional growth, and is a matter of maturity. The healthy human being is emotionally mature according to the age at the moment. Maturity gradually involves the individual in responsibility for environment.

Just as physical maturity is an extremely complex matter if one takes into account the whole of physiology (for instance, the bio-chemistry of muscle-tone) so is emotional maturity complex. It will be the main aim of this book gradually to indicate the ways in which emotional development has been found to be complex, yet capable of being investigated by scientific method.

INTELLECT AND   Intellectual development is not comparable
HEALTH   with that of psyche and soma. There is no meaning to the term intellectual health.
The intellect like the psyche is dependent on the functioning of one special bodily organ, the brain (or certain parts of the brain). The basis for intellect is therefore the quality of the brain, but the intellect can only be described in terms of plus or minus unless the brain is deformed or distorted by physical illness. Developmentally the intellect itself cannot be ill, though it can be exploited by an ill psyche. The psyche, by contrast, can be ill itself, that is to say distorted by emotional developmental failures, in spite of a healthy brain basis for its functioning. The part of the brain on which the intellectual capacity depends is much more variable than that on which the psyche depends, being also a later arrival in racial evolution. Heredity and chance provide a brain that is below or above average in capacity for functioning, or chance or disease or accident (as for instance damage

sustained during the birth process) provide a brain that is deficient or damaged; or an infective process during childhood (meningitis, encephalitis) or a tumour cause patchy residual interferences with brain functioning; or in the treatment (so-called) of mental disorder the neuro-surgeon deliberately cuts the brain about in order to disturb strongly organised defences against madness, defences that themselves constitute a painful clinical state. In any of these ways the intellect is affected or the mental processes are modified, although the body (apart from the brain) may remain healthy. In all cases, however, the health or ill-health of the psyche needs to be assessed. At one extreme a child with an intelligence quotient of 80 may be healthy in body, and may also show healthy emotional development – becoming indeed a valuable and interesting person, of good character and of reliable disposition, even capable of becoming a good marriage partner and parent. At the other extreme, a child of exceptional intellect (I.Q. 140 plus) though possibly talented and valuable, may, if the emotional development is disordered, be extremely ill, liable to psychotic breakdown, unreliable in character, and quite unlikely eventually to become a citizen with a home of his or her own.

It is now well known that in relatively healthy children the intelligence quotient, worked out as it is with exact allowance for chronological age, remains more or less constant. This is only another way of stating the fact that intellect depends fundamentally on brain tissue endowment. A description of the ways in which the I.Q. does not remain constant is no more than an enumeration of the ways in which there is a distortion of use of intellect, this distortion due on the one hand to disturbances of the emotional development and on the other to supervening brain tissue disease.

In any group of defective children there may be a few whose brain would allow for average or even superior ability, and for whom the correct diagnosis is childhood psychosis. The mental defect is then a symptom of early disturbance of emotional growth. This type of defect is not uncommon.

By contrast, the clinician meets with the child whose intellect is anxiety-driven and overworked, again as a result of emotional disorder (threat of confusion) and whose I.Q., which is high on test, comes down on the scale when, as a result of psycho-therapy or of a successful environment manipulation, the fear of chaos becomes less imminent.

Intellect, then, is not just like the body and the psyche. It is of different stuff, and it is not possible to say of intellect that health is maturity and maturity is health. In fact there is no direct link between the concepts of health and of intellect. In health the mind works at the level of brain functioning because the emotional development of the individual is satisfactory.

All this will need detailed consideration.

CHAPTER 2

ILL-HEALTH

A T THIS POINT it is useful to look at ill-health in a broad way. It is possible to make a fairly simple statement of diseases and disorders of both the soma and the psyche; the interaction of the two is complicated, but a description on a basis of an acceptance of the dichotomy can be attempted.

SOMATIC ILL-HEALTH

Hereditary	evidence appearing after birth, or later evidence before or at birth			

Congenital	during labour
	  abnormality causing birth difficulty
	at birth
	  accidents of birth process			

Intake deficiency (Elimination defects)	calorie, trace substances, vitamin	Persecution (failure of nurture)	All grades between	Self-induced
Accident	pure chance war	" "	" "	" "
Infestation Infection	pure chance	"	"	"
(Not yet understood)	New growth. Certain diseases, probably infections, (acute rheumatism, chorea, etc.)			

This covers ill-health except for the vast category: body tissue functions disturbed by various psychological states.

It is perhaps surprising that so simple a statement can cover the whole of the task of the somatic paediatrician, especially since in practice the task is onerous and the knowledge required is so vast.

PSYCHE ILL-HEALTH   There is no simple statement of psyche ill-health except that clinically it is always a disorder of emotional development, even when caused quite obviously by adverse environmental factors.*

Bodily health (including brain tissue functioning) being taken for granted, it is possible to classify psyche ill-health into neurosis and psychosis. In a case of neurosis, difficulties started to arise in the interpersonal relationships that belong to family life, the child being then 2–5 years old. In this 2–5 age period the child is able to be a whole person among whole persons, and is subject to powerful instinctual experiences based on love between persons. In neurosis the emotional development of the child (or adult) at the earliest stages was within normal limits.

Psychosis is the name given to states of illness that started to develop at earlier dates, that is to say, before the child had become a whole person related to whole persons.

This crude classification is of limited usefulness, and as soon as a closer examination of psychotic clinical states is made the need arises for a more delicate method. At this point it is only necessary to draw attention to the value of taking into consideration the point of origin of the disturbances of emotional development, at the same time attempting to use the accepted psychiatric terms.

Thus:

---

* *Note for revision:* Add statement of health in terms of freedom from rigidity of defences.
Do you like him or her?   Yes   = health
Are you bored?   Yes   = ill-health

TYPE	CLINICAL STATE	ORIGIN
NEUROSES	Defensive organisations against anxiety: phobias, conversion hysteria, obsessional neurosis, etc.	Anxiety arising out of the instinctual life, as between persons.
PSYCHOSES		

	Manic-depressive
	    Depression
	    Contra-depressive defences
		Concern about ruthless love. Reaction to loss of objects.

	Persecution: from within
	    Hypochondria
	        from without
	    Defence by paranoia
	        withdrawal to inner world
		Concern about results of aggression.

SCHIZOPHRENIA	Defence by splitting
	        by disintegration
	        by loss of reality
	            sense
	        by loss of contact
		Failure of active adaptation by mother at early stage.

A rough statement of this kind gives the student a jumping off ground for the study of psyche illness in terms of adult psychiatry. It is more logical, however, to approach adult psychiatry from an intimate study of child psychiatry.

We shall find, in spite of our good intentions, that we shall need to develop a new classification, and in the end we shall not be satisfied.*

Clinically even ill children are neither all the time anxious nor all the time mad. Ordinarily we are confronted with successfully organised defences against anxiety, and in making a diagnosis we are concerned with the type of defence, with the success or failure in defence. Also it is important to know the type of anxiety that threatens;

Note for revision: Adumbrate a return to classification in new form: i.e. dependence + family and social provision; cope/not cope.

for instance, the defences may be against fear of loss of penis, or loss of some important function associated with an instinct; the defences may likewise be against depression, that is to say, against a hopelessness belonging to guilt feelings that are either themselves unconscious or to do with unconscious matters; and again the defences may be against fear of lack of contact with external reality or against the fear of chaotic distintegration.

All this will need closer examination but the point here is that there does exist some justification for a rough classification of children's minor emotional disorders according to the type of illness the children would be likely to have if, under stress, they should break down and become frankly ill. Such classification makes it possible for me to make a preliminary examination of the interaction of physical and psychiatric disorders, after which I return to the detailed study of emotional growth. For the present I must omit the failures of environment at the various stages, a subject that will also need detailed consideration later on in the book. Also, the antisocial type of symptomatology cannot be included at this stage.

CHAPTER 3

INTER-RELATIONSHIP OF
BODY DISEASE AND
PSYCHOLOGICAL DISORDER

THE EFFECT OF THE BODY AND ITS HEALTH ON THE PSYCHE

HEREDITY

IN THE CONSIDERATION of heredity there is not much room for confusion. Presumably all heredity is physical, even when the result is psychological (for instance, a tendency towards a depressive or a hysterical temperament passed on from parent to child). The basis of psyche is soma, and in evolution the soma came first. The psyche begins as an imaginative elaboration of physical functioning, having as its most important duty the binding together of past experiences, potentialities, and the present moment awareness, and expectancy for the future. Thus the self comes into existence. The psyche has of course no existence apart from brain and brain functioning.

Inheritance of personality traits and tendencies towards psychiatric types and disorders belongs to the physical, and limits are set to psycho-therapy by inheritance. These limits are relatively unimportant in the treatment of neurotic disorder, more important in the treatment of psychotic disorder, and most important of all in the psycho-analysis of the healthy, that is to say, of those who are (by definition) the nearest to being what they came into the world equipped to be.

It is to be noted that certain inherited disease tendencies appear clinically at a late date, so that, though inherited, they are not congenital.

CONGENITAL DISORDER   Heredity concerns factors that existed
                       before conception. Congenital disorders are
                       those that are evident by the end of the
                       birth process.

The term congenital refers to two sets of disorder, firstly those
diseases and disabilities that exist before the date of the birth, in the
intra-uterine period, and those that are sequelae of the birth process
itself.

The *paediatrician* will think in terms of growth deficiencies
(example, mental defect due to maternal German measles in the
second month of pregnancy), orthopaedic deformities (example, dislo-
cated hip, club foot), infections derived from the mother (example,
syphilis before birth and gonorrhoea during birth), blood incompati-
bility between mother and baby, injury to meninges or even to brain
due to birth delays (maternal small pelvis, excessive asphyxia during
prolonged labour), and so on. The paediatrician has a wide field here
for his highly specialised work, and he cannot be expected to be
concerned with the birth experiences (psychological) of undeformed
healthy infants who are neither asphyxiated nor shocked in the physical sense.

In recent years the *gynaecologist* has become interested in the
psychology of birth, having almost achieved the first aim of making
parturition a safe physical experience. It is the psychology of the
mother that is mostly studied, however, and what is at present being
taught can almost be summed up in the words: freedom from fear.
This [is] to be brought about by truthful instruction, which makes
possible a state of relaxation in the mother. Personal confidence in one
doctor and one nurse remains the mother's main prop, although this is
not always mentioned. Neither the gynaecologist nor the maternity
nurse can be expected to show interest in the psychology of the infant
at about the time of being born. The mother herself is not in a good
position to become a pioneer just at this time of the birth of her baby.
Yet she knows the psychology of her baby must be considered. When
shall she find understanding? The psychologist must step in until the
paediatrician and the gynaecologist come round to a study of infant
psychology.

With the development of the brain as a functioning organ there starts a storing of experiences, and body memories that are personal begin to gather together to form a new human being. There is good evidence that the body movements of intra-uterine life have significance and presumably, in a silent manner, the restfulness of the womb-life also.

Somewhere about the time of birth a great awakening occurs, so that we note a difference between a baby born prematurely and one born post-maturely. The one is not yet ready for life and the other is liable to be born in a frustrated state, having been ready and kept waiting.

On the whole, however, the infant's own psychology does not affect the disorders collected together under the term "congenital". On the other hand the events of birth very much affect the psychology of the child. A study of this must be made after the reader has been introduced to the human being who is at the very beginning of life.

As soon as the infant is born the effect of infant psychology on bodily health at once becomes evident.

DEFICIENCIES OF INTAKE   The establishment of feeding is by no means all a matter of reflexes. It is well known that a mother's emotional state affects the baby's ability to take the breast, and it is also true that babies vary in their being easy or difficult to feed, even from the very beginning. There will be much to say about the psychology of the initiation of feeding and of its continuation. This is not in any way a detraction from the physical side of feeding, which is still being studied in great detail within the paediatric setting. For a study of this subject above all others there is a need for co-operation and understanding between those who know a great deal about the physical side (involving physiology, anatomy, neurology, biochemistry) and those who begin to know something about the psychological side. As an example that is instructive for the non-medical psychologist I would cite the rather rare condition known as "short oesophagus". This physical deformity causes feeding difficulties, and especially a tendency to vomit. Posture affects the symptomatology. In the course of time there is a tendency for the condition to right itself, so that whatever measures are being adopted at the time are given credit. These measures may easily be of the nature of advice as to management, or even psycho-therapy of the mother. Those who study infant psychology cannot afford to be ignorant of the physical disorders and their natural history, though mercifully they need not be competent to take over full responsibility for the physical side, which should be shared between the two types of specialist.

In the feeding disturbances of older infants the place of psychology becomes more and more self-evident. Infants can be normally faddy, and it may be an illness in an infant that leads to an acceptance of all food decently offered. We shall examine the reasons for this fact. In the extreme an infant of any age may, like an older child, become so actively inhibited as a feeder that the result is fatal. There is every grade in between healthy faddiness and pathological inhibition.

There is every kind of admixture of the physical and the psychological. A familiar example is that of the child with a congenital cleft palate, unable to enjoy feeding in the ordinary way and necessarily subjected to repeated operations, and separations from the mother. The infant's emotional development is affected, but not necessarily to a crippling extent, because the doctor and nurses can so easily see the sense in the infant's distress, with the result that they take steps to counteract the environmental disturbances. When the sense in infant distress generally is recognised, doctors and nurses will be able to do a great deal, apart altogether from acquiring specialised psychological knowledge, in the prevention of psychological illness of the kind that starts in infancy.

ELIMINATION DEFECTS   Here there is not much difficulty in sorting out the physical from the psychological.
Except in the rare case in which the excretory apparatus is deformed or diseased, disordered eliminatory functioning is frankly a matter of an emotional conflict appearing in body terms.

ACCIDENTS   Whereas at one end of the scale there is the operation of pure chance, at the other end is accident-proneness, a condition that belongs to the depression class of psychiatric disorder. Similarly, of those who get ill-treated, there are always some who carry a need to be persecuted, and this need for persecution, which is the basis of the psychiatric illness called paranoia, may start surprisingly early in infancy, in fact very soon after birth.

Of infections it can be said that some depend entirely on physical states, for example measles; a child who has not had measles catches it from someone who is starting the disease. Some infections on the other hand are influenced by emotional states. For instance, the course of phthisis can be closely related to the course of depression phases, although the surgical type of tuberculosis is not so related. Pneumonia, especially in the days before antibiotics, was very much a test of the will to live, and recovery therefore depended to a large extent on the nursing. In the old days nurses derived immense satisfaction from their successes with pneumonia patients because they knew they often saved life by their personal devotion. The nursing student of today loses much by the fact of the cure of pneumonia by relatively mechanical method.

A CATEGORY FOR THE NOT-YET-KNOWN   Nearly all the physical diseases can be fitted into these few categories. It is necessary to remind non-medical readers, however, that there are body diseases that really are physical, the cause of which is not yet understood. An example is "new growth".* Also rheumatic fever and chorea, which are common, are of cause unknown.

It does not mean that a disease is likely to be found to be psychological simply because the physical cause has not yet been made clear, and this is true in spite of the fact that rheumatic fever and especially chorea can at times seem to follow emotional shock or acute distress.

ALLERGY   More difficult to place is the collection of disorders that group under the heading "allergy". Those who are enthusiastic

---

* General term for cancer, that is to say, carcinoma, sarcoma, and probably lymphadenoma and leukaemia.

about allergy, or tissue over-sensitivity to various agents (such as pollen in hay-fever) claim to be able to explain a vast group of symptoms which most other observers would assume to be mainly psychological. An example is asthma. Asthma is a disturbance of body functioning which presumably can be caused by a purely physical sensitivity of bronchial muscle to inhaled substance. But an attack of asthma can be purely psychological, as anyone will agree who has a child with asthma under the close observation that goes with regular daily psycho-therapy (as in psycho-analysis). Asthma is a good example of the borderline disorder, and it is just as necessary to remind the psychological investigator that there is a physical predisposition, and that there is a relationship between asthma and infantile eczema, as it is to remind the somatic doctor that the illness is psychological.

Allergy turns out to be a vast distraction from main principles, and the usefulness of the term is chiefly in the matter of description of clinical states. Work on allergy which seemed to provide a promising line of attack on psyche-soma disorders has led to psychology rather than to physiology and biochemistry. I do not forget that asthma can be said to be a producer of psychiatric disorder, apart from the problem of its own causation in any one case, since it is impossible for a child or adult to suffer from asthma (whatever its cause) without becoming specifically orientated to it.

THE EFFECT OF THE PSYCHE ON THE BODY AND ITS FUNCTIONING

Healthy emotional development provides the child with a meaning to physical health, just as physical health provides a reassurance to the child that is of great value in emotional development.

The strains and stresses of normal emotional growth, and also some abnormal states of the psyche, have an adverse effect on the body.

Instinct-freedom promotes body health, and from this it follows that in normal development with increasing instinct control the body has to be sacrificed at many points, instinct-freedom being normally curtailed in the child's socialisation process. The principle to be remembered is that where a conflict in the psyche is relatively conscious the instincts are dealt with by self-control; compromise between the demands of instinct and those of external reality or society or conscience can be made with the least possible damage. On the other hand, where the conflict between impulse and Ego-ideal is in the repressed unconscious the resulting inhibitions and anxieties and compulsions are more blind, less capable of adaptation to circumstances, and more harmful to the body and to the body processes and functions.

The body of a child is capable of standing great strain, but exactly the same strain continued on into adult life may lead eventually to irreversible physical states, such as benign hypertension, ulceration of the mucosa of some portion of the digestive tract, thyroid gland over-action, etc.

The later stages of these irreversible body changes that have been initiated by conflict in the psyche need to be dealt with by the physician or surgeon or endocrinologist, and this is true *even when* at this late date psycho-therapy is successfully given. Psycho-therapy given successfully at an earlier date would have cut out the need for help from the physician or surgeon.

CHAPTER 4

THE PSYCHO-SOMATIC FIELD

I T IS TO PAEDIATRICS rather than to medicine applied to adults that we should look for elucidation of the problems of psycho-somatics. Children offer the best material for the study of the alterations in body tissues and in body functioning that are associated with or secondary to psychological phenomena.

Psycho-somatic medicine has become a branch of medical research and practice, one that is unfortunately cut off from all three of its close relations: psychiatry, general medicine and psycho-analysis. The reasons for this are like those that have led to the use of the terms mental and physical as if they describe opposed phenomena. Human nature is not a matter of mind and body – it is a matter of inter-related psyche and soma, with the mind as a flourish on the edge of psycho-somatic functioning.

Disorders of the psyche-soma are alterations of the body or of body functioning associated with psyche states. These alterations are best studied in the paediatric clinical field, not only because the conditions are simpler in children, but also because psyche states of adults cannot be understood without reference to the childhood of the subjects being investigated.

The basis of psycho-somatics is live anatomy, which is called physiology. The tissues are alive and they are part of a whole animal, and are affected by the varying psyche states of that animal.

The first complications to be studied are those physiological changes that belong to activity and rest; then the changes belonging to local and general excitements, the latter being characterised by the three phases of preparation, climax and recovery. In the study of general excitement the tissues cannot be studied apart from their relation to the total psyche. Once the total psyche has been accepted, then physiology is concerned with the changes specific to desire and to rage, and also to affectionate love, fear, anxiety, grief and other affects that are facets of elaborate fantasy, fantasy that is specific to the individual.

In all this work the student of the psyche-soma is concerned with conscious and unconscious fantasy that is, so to speak, the histology of the psyche, the imaginative elaboration of all somatic functioning that is specific to the individual. If two persons waggle a finger, for the anatomist and the physiologist there is an essential similarity in the two events. For the psyche-soma student, however, there must be added to the anatomy and the physiology of the action the meaning of the action to the individual, and because of this the waggling of the finger is specific in each case to the individual who waggles.

Somewhere therefore physiology merges gently into psycho-somatics, which includes the physiology of the somatic changes associated with strains and stresses of the psyche. First there are the controls that are inherent in the socialisation process, and then there are the controls and inhibitions that are pathological and associated with repression and unconscious conflicts in the psyche.

Lastly, in psycho-somatics one cannot assume a close association between the psyche and the soma; psycho-somatics must take into account the states both common and important in which the relationship between psyche and soma is loosened or lost.

Detailed study of psycho-somatic paediatrics cannot be made till after the full exposition of the emotional development of the human individual.

It will be seen that to understand these disorders that do indeed form a real though very wide clinical group one must touch on every kind and degree of psychological disorder and include the inner conflicts that are inherent in life, that are inherent in the management of instincts and in the personal compromise with impulse that belongs to the gradual socialisation of each human individual.

In health there are two main trends in psycho-somatic paediatrics: physical health: its effect on psyche functioning and development; psyche health: its effect on physical development and function.

In ill-health there are also two trends: physical ill-health: its effect on psyche development; psyche ill-health: its effect on physical development.

The understanding of any of these comes from the study of the developing physically healthy person, for it is only on the assumption of an *absence of physical disease* that so complex a study can be made at all. If absence of primary body disease is assumed, then the gradual interweaving of the body and psyche of one person can be examined, and certain basic principles can be formulated.

It is found that emotional development is normally painful and punctuated by conflict: the body must suffer on account of this, even though no diseases that are primarily physical exist.* In this way the study of psycho-somatic disorder must be through psychology, and through seeing the effect of psyche-troubles on the body part of the person. It must be that way round. Physicians do not like this. They would like to be able to apply their knowledge of body illness directly to psycho-somatic disorder. But it cannot be done. The natural way is the study of psycho-somatic disorder in the child (or adult) who is free from any physical disease or physical limitation. Only later, after the principle has been understood, can there be understanding of body diseases and their effect on the psyche. It can be seen that physical medicine is a country with boundaries that are artificially maintained in order to limit the doctor's obligation. Physical medicine merges naturally into psycho-somatics.

The psyche part of the person is concerned with relationships, relationships within, relationships to the body, to the external world. Arising out of what may be called the imaginative elaboration of body functioning of all kinds and the accumulation of memories, the psyche (specifically dependent on brain functioning) binds the experienced past, the present and the expected future together, makes sense of the person's sense of self, and justifies our perception of an individual there in that body.

The psyche, developing in this way, becomes something that has a

---

* *Note for revision:* Be sure of the slant: psycho-somatic disorder with its positive sense of countering the flight to ⸺ intellect,
                                                    depersonalised states.

position from which to become related to external reality, becomes a thing with a capacity to create and to perceive external reality, becomes a qualitatively enriched being able to go further than can be explained by environmental influences, and able not only to adapt but also to refuse to adapt, and becomes a creature with what feels like a capacity for choice.

None of this appears automatically as a growth phenomenon. There is indeed an inherent growth element, but the early dependence on an adaptive environment is so great that this factor of growth becomes overlaid. In bodily development the growth factor is more clear; in the development of the psyche, by contrast, there is a possibility of failure at every point, and indeed there can be no such thing as growth without distortion due to some degree of failure of environmental adaptation.

Psycho-somatic development is a gradual achievement, and has its own speed, and if the term maturity be allowed an age-reference then maturity is health and health is maturity. The whole process of development must be carried through, each gap or jump in development is a distortion, and a hurry here or a delay there each leaves a scar.

Moreover there is nothing to be gained by wrangling over the date at which psycho-somatic paediatrics, or human nature itself starts. The only certain date is that of conception. The date of birth is obviously notable, but much has happened before, especially in the post-mature infant, and at birth there is already an individuality which is so striking that in a case of identical twins experienced nurses are immediately conscious of exceptional similarity. By the end of two weeks any baby has had plenty of things happen that are entirely personal. At the age at which an adoption becomes relatively easy to arrange each baby has been so stamped with actual experience that the adopting parents have a problem of management that is essentially different from that which they would have had if the infant had been their own and in their own care from the start.

PART II

THE EMOTIONAL DEVELOPMENT
OF THE HUMAN BEING

Introduction

THE PRELIMINARY examination of the scope of psycho-somatic paediatrics has only shown the need for an understanding of the emotional development of the individual. On the somatic side the paediatrician bases everything on anatomy and physiology, and on the psyche side there must be an equivalent discipline. Academic psychology does not supply the answer. The only answer is dynamic psychology, or in other words psycho-analysis.

It will now be necessary to examine the development of the psyche–soma, which, with mind functioning, gradually becomes the individual self-conscious person, a person not only related to environment but eventually taking part in the maintenance and re-creation of that environment. An absence of primarily physical disease will be assumed, up to the point near the end when it is considered that an inclusion of this further complication is in place.

Average brain tissue endowment is also assumed, since mental defect and idiocy are physical defects with secondary psychological features. Purposely, for the time being, mind is being left out of account except in so far as it is what I have called a flourish at the edge of the psyche–soma.

It would be logical to give a description of the developing human being starting at conception, gradually working through intra-uterine life, birth, the primitive and less primitive stages of emotional growth, passing in review the toddler and the child in the latency period, and the adolescent, and eventually reaching the mature adult who is ready to take a place in the world, and who grows old and so dies.

I have chosen to start with the period of the first maturity, with the child at the late-toddler stage at which interpersonal relationships have come to have full meaning, and I have chosen this way because I can take for granted in the reader a certain familiarity with Freud's work which traces the origin of neurotic illness in adults to the conflicts arising in the individual during this era.

From a statement of the dynamic psychology of early childhood I shall proceed backwards, reaching further and further back into the unknown of the earliest moments at which the term human being can be applied to the foetus in the womb. Afterwards it will be possible to go forward and to examine the special characteristics of the latency period and of adolescence.

My presentation of dynamic psychology will therefore be broken up in the following way:

(a) Interpersonal relationships and attendant complications.

(b) The achievement of a personal unit and the capacity for concern.

(c) The primitive tasks of
  (1) Integration of self.
  (2) Psycho-somatic *modus vivendi*.
  (3) Reality contact through illusion.

The reader is asked to remember, when reading one part of my statement, that the other parts are being deliberately excluded, and are not forgotten. The language of one part is the wrong language for another part.

It is a highly artificial procedure, this dissection out of stages of development. In fact the human child is all the time at all stages, even although one stage can be said to dominate. The primitive tasks are never completed, and throughout childhood their incompleteness presents a challenge to the parent and the educator, though originally they belong to the realm of infant care. Similarly the burdens that come to the psyche at the changeover from ruthlessness to concern and when there comes a capacity to join together past, present, and future also very much interest parents and educators of children of all ages, although initially they belong to those who care for the infant who is just about becoming ready to be "weaned", to be able to deal with loss without quite losing what is (in one sense only) lost.

Curiously enough it is these early-starting problems rather than the subject matter of my first section that are of most interest to the reader of a book on psychology. The later troubles of the more mature child who has reached the complications and enrichments of interpersonal relationships are by their very nature more a matter of private concern to each child and are less and less (as the child matures) a part of the child's dependence. It is maddening and not useful for a parent or educator to be told (though quite rightly) that a child's symptom is a matter of repression, that the cause of neurotic disturbance is something that is essentially in the unconscious, and that the only thing that can be done is to give the child psycho-therapy (which in any case is probably unavailable or too expensive).

It is not just a "resistance" on the part of parents and teachers that makes them impatient with the truths that are formulated in Oedipus Complex terms. These facts (that belong principally to the first section of my description) tend to make people feel helpless. What can they do? By contrast, the needs of a child that are residual from infancy present the parent and teacher with problems that they themselves can treat, by emphasis of some or other aspect of ordinary child care and education.

Nevertheless it will be conceded that an understanding of what is going on inside the child of 4 can be helpful even when no action on the part of the adult in charge can cure a presenting symptom. Understanding of the human child is deficient if it stops short at the limits of the infant tasks and needs. It is certainly valuable to a child in the throes of the Oedipus Complex to be understood, even if such understanding leads to sympathy rather than to useful action.

CHAPTER I

INTERPERSONAL RELATIONSHIPS

T HE FIRST PART of this study of human psychology, that dealing with interpersonal relationships, derives directly from the well-known work of the last fifty years which has the treatment of neurosis as its basis. The ideas are almost entirely derived from Freud or from those applying his method which he called psycho-analysis. All that I have to say has already been stated in the vast literature now available; nevertheless it is not possible for me to shirk making a statement in my own language, so that the reader may get the whole subject reviewed by one person.

This is the part of psycho-analytic theory that becomes taken for granted by all psycho-analysts; it is that which enables analysts of widely divergent views on modern developments of theory and practice to feel united fundamentally, so that the Institute of Psycho-Analysis, composed as it is of all psycho-analysts, can set up and work a training scheme in this country and can give a qualification to practise. There is this basis of theory that can be taught to students before they are introduced to the matters that are more clearly research problems.

Almost every aspect of relationships between whole persons was touched on by Freud himself, and in fact it is very difficult now to contribute except by fresh statement of what is accepted. Freud did the unpleasant things for us, pointing out the reality and force of the unconscious, getting to the pain, anguish, conflict which invariably lie at the root of symptom formations, also putting forward, arrogantly if necessary, the importance of instinct and the significance of childhood sexuality. Any theory that denies or bypasses these matters is unhelpful.

The idea of the developing child dominates and rightly dominates the teaching of childhood psychology, the idea of emotional development intertwined with bodily growth. Because of this it is never profitable to study a *state of affairs* in psychology; as in history the state of affairs at any one moment has a past and a future belonging to it. This is an observation of fundamental importance and by following this principle the psycho-analyst has broken away from the shackles of academic psychology and of mental hospital psychiatry and of general medicine.

The present statement of the psychology of the small child takes for granted healthy development prior to the point at which it can be said: this child is now a whole human being, related to whole human beings. We know that it is somewhat artificial to take so much for granted. We know also that there is no point in time at which such a description suddenly applies. Any stage in development is reached and lost and reached and lost over and over again; the attainment of a stage in development only gradually becomes fact, and then only under certain conditions. These conditions gradually become less vitally important but perhaps never become negligible. But it is necessary to make this assumption of previous developmental success. The more complex must develop out of the more simple.

A claim that the healthy child can be completely understood on the basis of a study of neurosis and its origins in childhood would be absurd. Not quite so absurd would be a claim that a good way to study the healthy child, *assuming healthy infancy development*, is through the understanding of symptom formation of neurotic type. The reason is that the defences organised in neurosis point the way to the anxiety which not only underlies the neurotic symptom but also gives force and quality to the manifestations of health.

In analysis of adults the origin of neurotic symptoms can be regularly traced back to the time of strain and stress in the period before latency, when the adult was a child of 2–5 years. We turn therefore to the child of this age for our first glimpse of what is going on in the course of emotional development.

An argument in terms of theoretical extremes could be used to confound this method of procedure. At one extreme is the perfect infancy, which is the basis for a perfect childhood, free from neurotic disturbance. At the other extreme is a distorted infancy, the distortions making impossible a normal or healthy growth at any later stage. It might be asked: where then is the child who is building up defences of neurotic quality? In between the extremes, and commonly, we find relatively healthy small children with a certain liability to neurotic illness which can be kept in check by suitable management, and also small children with a rather strong liability to neurotic illness, who will certainly not be brought through without some symptom organisation, and yet who will pass for healthy. These latter are especially dependent on a continuing stable emotional environment. It should be added that between the latter and the children in the category labelled psychotic are those who present illness of deceptively neurotic type but who, under treatment, reveal so much fundamental disorder of infantile emotional development that the term psychosis is gradually found to be more appropriate.

Infancy	2–5 years
1. Perfect infancy	– making neurotic distortions at this stage unlikely
2. Imperfect infancy	– giving a basis for neurotic anxiety
3. Distorted infancy development	– making neurotic disturbance likely
4. Distorted infancy development	– neurotic overlay of psychotic quality that is revealed in course of psycho-therapy or in periods of "breakdown"
5. Distorted infancy development	– giving insufficient health at this stage for the development of illness of neurotic quality, i.e. infantile psychosis already a fact

It will be understood that hereditary factors play right across this classification, and disturb and distort any neatness which may have crept in.

The relatively healthy (mature for age) infant passes on into the stage of being a whole person who is self-conscious and conscious of other selves. There is a tremendous amount in the daily life of such a child that must now be ignored because it belongs to the persistence of the infantile (of any and every stage) and is therefore not under discussion.

THE FAMILY   The arrival of the child at a stage in development at which the child can appreciate at one moment the existence of three persons, the self and two others, is met in most cultures by the provision of the family setting. In the family the child can go step by step from the three-body relationship to relationships of all degrees of complexity. It is the simple triangle that presents the difficulties, and the full richness of human experience. In the family setting the two parents can also supply continuity in time, perhaps continuity from the child's conception right through to the end of the dependence that characterises the end of adolescence.

INSTINCT   The clue to healthy early childhood (with the reservations which have been made about important infantile residues) is INSTINCT. For this reason a close study of instinct and its development is necessary.

Instinct is the term given to the powerful biological drives which come and go in the life of the infant or child, and which demand action. The stirrings of instinct cause the child, like any other animal, to make preparations for satisfaction of the full-blown instinct when it eventually reaches a climax of demand. If satisfaction can be provided at the climax of demand, then there is a reward of pleasure and also a temporary relief from instinct. Incomplete or ill-timed satisfaction results in incomplete relief, discomfort, and an absence of a much-needed resting period between waves of demand. In this statement there is not much difference according to the type of instinctual demand, nor is there much difference between human beings and animals. It is not necessary here to enter into a discussion about classification of instincts, nor even to decide whether there is one instinct, or whether there are two or perhaps scores of instincts. All this is irrelevant.

In the human infant and child there is an IMAGINATIVE ELABORATION of all body functioning (providing there is a functioning brain) and this is so much more true of children than of the most interesting of animals, that it is *never* safe to carry an argument over from animal psychology to human. It is for this reason that animal psychology is actually misleading unless very carefully applied to the consideration of human problems.

It is valuable in considering instinctual excitement to take into account the body function most powerfully involved. The excited part may be the mouth, the anus, the urinary tract, the skin, one or other part of the male or female genitals, the nasal mucous membrane, the breathing apparatus, or the musculature generally, or the ticklish groins or armpits.

Excitement is local and general, and general excitement can be said both to contribute to the child's sense of being a whole being and also to depend on the child's achievement of integration in the course of development.

A climax of a kind may be reached almost anywhere, but more specifically in certain parts.

Some organisations of excitement are found to be dominant, and the imaginative elaboration of all excitements tends to be in terms of the dominant instinct type. It is rather obvious that for a small infant the intake apparatus is dominant, and *oral erotism* coloured by ideas of oral type is generally accepted as characteristic of the first stage of instinct development.

(It is to be remembered that all the other things that could be said about infants are not being said at this stage by deliberate decision, for purposes of clear presentation.)

There is a progression of instinct type during infancy, culminating in the dominance of genital erotic excitement and the fantasy which characterises the toddler age child who has developed fully at all the infantile levels. In between the first or oral stage and the last or genital there is a variable experience of other functions and development of appropriate fantasy. The anal or urethral functions with appropriate fantasy may dominate in a transitional way, or may come to dominate permanently, thus predetermining a character-type.

There is a progression of instict dominance according to the function involved and according also to the fantasy:

Pregenital
Phallic
Genital

First the infant with all manner of excitements, and perhaps localised genital excitement, but not yet with fantasy of genital quality. Here male and female are not necessarily unalike.

Second, intermediate stage with the male genital as a central theme, with its erection and periodic sensitisation. Here the female state is a negative matter, and the existence of this stage marks the parting of the ways between the boy and girl infant.

Third the genital stage, in which fantasy has become enriched to include all that in adolescence reappears as male and female action (penetration, being penetrated; impregnation, being impregnated; etc.).

At one time it was thought that this idea of progression from pregenital to phallic and genital could be applied in the early stages so that the pregenital stage was itself divided up:

pregenital   oral   oral erotic (suck)
                    oral sadistic (bite)
             anal   anal erotic (defaecation)
                    anal sadistic (control)
             with
             urethral erotic and sadistic
             as a variable alternative

Even a further breaking up of stages was attempted (Abraham). Certainly it would be unwise to throw away the whole of this work on the theory of infantile instinct life. Nevertheless it is necessary now for me to take into account later work in its effect on this part of theory in spite of the fact that for the moment I am deliberately excluding other modes of presentation.

The objections are as follows:

(1) There is no certainty that the fantasy of oral activity is at first erotic (i.e. without sadism, or pre-ambivalent) and then sadistic, destructive and, so to speak, ambivalent. It is better to say that it is the infant who changes, starting ruthless and then becoming concerned. The ambivalence has to do with the Ego changes in the infant rather than with Id (or instinct) development.

(2) The anal stage is extremely variable and can therefore hardly be given status equivalent to that of the oral and genital. For instance, for one infant anal experience is the erotic one associated with defaecation at the exciting moment; for another there is displaced oral erotism in anal receptive experience, perhaps through anal manipulations; for another the main element is control, either because of training, or because of anal pain (fissure) or because of deprivation (loss of the right place for defaecation).

(3) Anal experience, like urethral, is dominated by the idea of excretion of stuff; and this stuff has a prehistory; it has been inside, and it was originally a by-product of oral experience. Therefore anal (and urethral) experience is much more than a stage in Id growth, so much so that it cannot exactly be classified and timed. Nevertheless it is true enough that within the Id growth classification labelled pregenital, the oral quality precedes the various anal qualities (and urethral).

Skin erotism cannot be brought into this scheme of things since it is partly a spread out from the oral and the anal and the urethral, and an over-emphasis on skin involves Ego distress, which is not under discussion in this part of my exposition.

The reader must form a personal opinion in these matters, after learning what is taught as far as possible in the historical manner, which is the only way that the theory of any one moment becomes intelligible and interesting.

I personally prefer the following useful chart, which however does not keep to the point, since it goes beyond Id growth to Ego development.

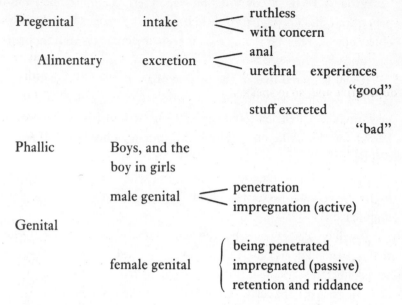

Pregenital	intake	⟨ ruthless / with concern
Alimentary	excretion	⟨ anal / urethral experiences
		"good"
	stuff excreted	
		"bad"

Phallic	Boys, and the boy in girls	
	male genital	⟨ penetration / impregnation (active)
Genital		
	female genital	{ being penetrated / impregnated (passive) / retention and riddance

It will be seen that the female side of human nature calls on the pregenital in a way that the male side need not do in phases of mature genital experience.

There is something inherently unsatisfactory in this attempt to classify pregenital instincts. This has to do with the fact that we are trying to look back at infancy from the toddler stage, and not to look at the infant. But at the moment we are doing this on purpose. We are trying to keep to the task of examining the toddler who has come through infancy in a healthy way, and who is now concerned with instinctual experiences of genital type, noting that the genital type of instinct develops out of the pregenital and that it shows traces of its inheritance in health, and distortions related to such inheritance in ill-health.

In the imaginative elaboration of genital functions the continued importance of the pregenital shows itself; yet it is probably possible to give a clear-cut distinction between the fantasy of experience of the phallic and genital respectively in the boy (and the boy in girls). In the first phase the fact of erection is the important thing, the idea being that here is something important, loss of which would be terrible. The

erection and sensitisation comes either in direct relation to an actively
loved person or with ideas of rivalry, with a loved person in the
background. In the second phallic stage there is a more open aim of
penetration and impregnation, and here a real person is likely to be the
object of love. How far that person is seen objectively is another matter
that must be discussed later.

It will be noted that in the phallic phase the child's performance
(swank) is in line with the fantasy, whereas in the genital the child's
performance is deficient, and the child must wait (till puberty as we
know) for the ability to act out the dream. This is an important
distinction, since it implies that at the genital phase the child's Ego is
able to deal with a tremendous quantity of frustration. Fear of castration
by the rival father becomes welcome as an alternative to the agony of
impotence.

It will be seen at once that the genital phase gathers to itself much
that is pregenital, and also much that cannot be described in the terms
now deliberately adopted. But here the important fact is that of erection
occurring as part of a relationship and having associated with it ideas of
making irreversible changes in the body of the loved person.

The development of the small child's ideas about the vagina is much
affected by cultural pattern. The boy's idea of the vagina is given by his
own oral (and anal) desires, and also by something corresponding
exactly to vaginal sensation and longing for which the appropriate desire
seems to exist in boys although the actual opening is absent.

In the case of girls there is much more than in boys of a leaning
back on the pregenital while the full genital and pregnancy and
breast-feeding capacity is as yet a matter of the distant future except in
dream and play. This is associated with a capacity for identification
with mother and with woman, and in cultures which early cater for this
capacity for identification (way of squatting and so on) the "boy in the
girl" can seem to be absent. But the male in the female is always
present and important, and the result is a sequence of ideas which
could be put into the following words:

> I have a penis. Of course I shall grow a penis. I had a penis, I am
> traumatised (punishment for excitement). I shall use a penis by

proxy, let a male act for me. I shall let the male use me. In this way I get a deficiency made up but acknowledge a dependence on the male for completeness.* Through this I discover my true female genital.

In this way the female child may come round in adolescence or in adult life to being able to be a woman, but the route is a precarious one and offers much opportunity for development along homosexual lines etc. By this way of describing female sexuality one sees that there is plenty of room for unhappiness and distress in small girls who simply feel inferior when their brothers swank, and who try to make up for inferiority by using their whole body as a representative of the phallus, or by finding a phallus instead of a baby in the doll.† There is instability in all solutions, however, which take for granted the loss of a penis in the female or the supremacy of the male on account of his phallus.

Our culture tends to foster this belief especially by not giving a name and specific importance to the little girl's genital mouth. There is no English word actually for the male genital, but there are innumerable terms in common usage in the nursery.‡ In the nursery, however, there is usually no verbal recognition of the vagina.

Imaginative identification with the male enriches the girl's appreciation of the man's function and eventually strengthens her personal relation to a chosen man.

Certainly in the analysis of neurosis in women the full recognition of penis envy is necessary. Penis envy may be very difficult to get at, just where it is most powerfully operative. It may be most difficult in the case of a woman who has no consciousness of penis envy whatever at the start of a treatment, and who has a powerfully developed female sexuality based on female genital functioning, which has perhaps

---

* At the phallic phase a boy is complete, and at the genital he is dependent on the female for completeness.

† *Note for revision:* Corresponding male envy of female to be stated.

‡ It would be wrong to think that this is no more than a cultural neurosis, however. A culture in which the little girl is allowed to know the woman's function from very early is not thereby necessarily the girl's best friend.

enabled her to have already been a satisfactory wife and to have had a family of children, and perhaps grandchildren.

Penis envy as a powerful drive in girls and women cannot be ignored, but in spite of this there is undoubtedly a basic female sexuality and fantasy which starts from very early in infancy. The vagina probably becomes active and excitable in association with feeding during infancy and with anal experiences, and the true female genital functioning tends to be hidden, if not actually secret. Sometimes the genital erotism element becomes exaggerated (as in the compulsive masturbation that can be associated with deprivation even at a very early age, even producing marked hypertrophy of the vulva) but usually the type of fantasy is of collecting and of secrecy and of hiding. In anal terms there is a reluctance to part with faeces and in urinary terms a tendency to retention, but in genital terms the ideas find fullest expression through identification with mother or with older girls who are able to experience and to conceive. The little girl's play, in so far as she is truly female, is of type that shows a mothering tendency, and the actual genital functioning is not so much in evidence as that of the male (in both boys and girls). On the other hand there is more hurting in the male dream or game than in the female.

The game: can you keep a secret? belongs typically to the female side of human nature, just as fighting and pushing things into holes belongs to the male side. Unless a girl can keep a secret she cannot become pregnant. Unless a boy can fight or push a train through a tunnel he cannot deliberately impregnate. In the games of small children we get a glimpse of the imaginative elaboration of their dominant bodily functionings, especially in an analytic treatment in which we get into very intimate contact with the child's psychic reality through the child's play and speech.

Readers of psycho-analytic literature may easily become impatient if they take some statement of analytic theory and treat it as if it were a final pronouncement, never to be modified. Psycho-analytic theory is all the time developing, and it must develop by a natural process rather like the emotional condition of the human being that is under study. There is no better example of the need for a historical perspective in the reading of psycho-analytic theory than that which relates to the early roots of female genitality.*

The study of psycho-neurosis shows that it is impossible to bypass penis envy and the "castrated male" fantasy in a statement of the developing girl child. But a couple of decades ago from a study of the literature it might have been thought that psycho-analytic theory had no place for any other kind of statement of female genitality than that of the female as a castrated male.

The fact is that the kind of statement of the progression of Id growth that is being attempted in this section is more suitable for the description of the male than of the female element. The female function and fantasy draw much more heavily on pregenital roots, and there is perhaps more room for a merging of individual girl children into the category *woman* than there is for a merging of boys into the category *man*.† Moreover, for a description of female sexuality it is necessary to be familiar with the child's developing fantasy about the inside both of herself and of the mother, and this belongs to another mode of presentation, one which will be attempted under the heading of "the depressive position in emotional development". For these reasons any statement of female sexuality here must be less complete as a description of girls than a statement here of male sexuality can be as a description of boys.

This remains, however: that in health, somewhere at about 1 ½–2 years, the small girl, just like the small boy, is reaching a stage which merits description in terms of interpersonal relationships, with instincts involved, instincts that have passed through the pregenital phases and have become genital both in their body localisation and their type fantasy. The little girl has a man in mind when genitally excited, and it is his penis that is genitally desired.

---

* See Jones, Ernest: (1927) "The Early Development of Female Sexuality" and Freud, Sigmund: (1931) *Female Sexuality*.

† I suggest that the three women that turn up in myths and dreams have no exact counterpart in three men. In the intercourse idea each man is specifically himself at that moment, whereas in the case of the girl there is a sense in which the unit is not a girl but a trio: female infant, veiled bride, and old woman. This is a vast subject in itself, not appropriate for study here.

The female in the boy (as well as the male in him) is also fundamental, although variable according to heredity, environmental influences belonging to the personal setting, and the more general cultural pattern. Distinction must be drawn between the little boy's capacity for identification with woman in respect of female genitality, and his capacity for identification with woman in her role of mother. The latter is more acceptable than the former in our culture; also it is less disturbing in the individual to the male genitality because it concerns the type of fantasy rather than localisation of body functioning.*

It is generally accepted that there is a bisexuality of all human beings, especially where fantasy is concerned, and in capacity for identification. The principal factor which determines the way a child grows is the sex of the person the child is in love with at the critical age, that is to say the period that is now being considered, after infancy and before the latency period. It is extremely convenient when the sexuality of a child develops principally along the lines of bodily endowment, that is to say, when a boy is mainly male, and a girl mainly female. However, society gains much if it can tolerate the homosexual as well as the heterosexual in the emotional development of children. A strong mother-identification in boys, and even girlishness, can have value when character development is in other respects satisfactory. A certain maleness in girls is not only tolerated, but is expected and valued.

LOVE RELATIONSHIPS   An examination of the other phenomena that characterise this stage of growth can now be made.

The basis of everything is the love that develops between child and other persons. These persons gradually become perceived as persons, but this does not mean they are objectively perceived to a full extent. Some children early get to know people much as they are, whereas others are more subjective, and hardly see except in so far as they are

---

* *Note for revision:* Make sure it is clear about normal homosexuality and oral erotism displaced to anus in homosexuality (manifest).

ready to imagine. The more subjective child risks less if the mother-figure should change; the less subjective child gains through appreciation of the actual qualities of various people, but risks more, stands to suffer more severely as a result of loss.

If health is thought of in terms of an absence of neurotic illness (absence of psychotic illness being assumed) then health is established in the management of the first triangular relationships, with the child power-driven by the newly established instincts of genital quality characteristic of the 2–5 year period. It is in this way that I personally interpret Freud's Oedipus Complex for boys and whatever corresponds to this in girls (inverted Oedipus Complex, Electra Complex, etc.). I think something is lost if the term "Oedipus Complex" is applied to the earlier stages, in which there are only two persons involved and the third person or part object is internalised, a phenomenon of inner reality. I cannot see value in the use of the term Oedipus Complex where one or more of the trio is a part object. In the Oedipus Complex, for me at least, each of the three of the triangle is a whole person, not only for the observer but also and especially for the child.

In this way the term "Oedipus Complex" has economic value in the description of the first interpersonal relationship with instincts in charge. Both fantasy and body functioning are included. In the fantasy the aim is the sexual union of mother and son, which involves *death*, the death of the father. Punishment comes in the form of castration of the child represented symbolically, as by blindness in the ancient myth. Castration anxiety is that which enables the child to continue to live, or to allow the father to live. The symbolic castration brings relief, and the blindness in the myth conveys the idea of what we now call the "repressed unconscious". By castration and suffering the son eventually attains psychological release, whereas if he had been killed he would not have suffered and he would not have been in a position to come through to a solution, so that the tragedy would have been futile or unproductive, mere dramatics.*

It is wise not to lean too heavily on the Electra myth, since the

---

* Oedipus comes through eventually, in the myth, to . . .

question must first be asked: is it to be brought in to illustrate female sexuality developing in a masculine way, with penis envy and castration complex as central themes, or that developing more directly out of identification and rivalry with the mother and the imaginative elaboration of specifically female genital organ functioning? If a term must be found, that of "inverted Oedipus Complex" is less harmful since it only claims that there is another way round for the girl, and leaves to the imagination all that there may be in the development of the theme.

The Oedipus Complex is thus a description of an achievement of health. Ill-health belongs not to the Oedipus Complex, but to the repression of ideas and inhibitions of functions that follow from the painful conflict that is expressed in the term ambivalence, as, for example, when a boy finds he hates and wants to kill and fears the father that he loves and trusts, because he is in love with his father's wife. Happy and healthy is the boy who reaches just exactly this in his emotional and physical development when the family is intact, and who can be seen through the awkward situations in the first instance by his own two parents that he knows well, parents who tolerate ideas, and whose inter-relationship is sound enough so that they do not fear the strain of loyalties brought about by the child's loves and hates.

When this stage is reached in a relatively open manner (assuming healthy development at earlier stages) the child is able to reach the most tremendous human feelings without excessive organisation of defences against anxiety. Yet defences there will always be, and these lead to the appearance of symptoms. Neurotic symptoms are organisations of defence against anxiety, in fact castration anxiety, anxiety which arises out of the inherent death wishes of the Oedipus Complex. The abnormal points to the normal.

CHAPTER 2

The concept of health
using instinct theory

W E H A V E N O W reached a position from which we can get a glimpse of the nature of the small child, of the meaning of health, and of the various factors, both internal and external, that inherently complicate the basic process of continuing development.

IMAGINATIVE
ELABORATION OF
FUNCTION

The basis of healthy development is bodily growth, also the change of infantile organ functioning that occurs with change of age; this carries a change of emphasis, as from alimentary to genital dominance. The imaginative elaboration of body functioning becomes organised into fantasy which is qualitatively determined by the body localisation but which is specific to the individual because of heredity and experience. According to whether the emphasis is on intake or excretion or on the genital excitement, so the preparation for orgiastic experience is dependent on the type of fantasy that will dominate at the moment of climax, whether this be orgasm or orgiastic.

The imaginative elaboration of function must be considered to exist at every degree of nearness to the physical functioning itself and at every degree of distance from its physical orgasm. The word unconscious according to one of its meanings* refers to near-physical fantasy, that which is least available to consciousness. At the other end of the scale is awareness of self, and of personal capacity for orgiastic or functional experience. I do not claim to be able to state this satisfac-

---

* Freud, Anna: (1936) *The Ego and the Mechanisms of Defence.*

torily. It will be remembered that in this section I am not delving into the problems of the building up of the self, but am taking for granted that the self has come into existence.

Even when the early phases of emotional development have been satisfactory there is still needed a long period of steady environment in which the personality can come to terms with itself at all levels of consciousness.

THE PSYCHE Out of the material of the imaginative elaboration of body functioning (which itself depends on the capacity and healthy functioning of one organ: the brain) the psyche is forged. It can safely be said that fantasy that is near to body functioning is dependent on the function of the part of the brain that is less modern in evolution, whereas self-awareness is dependent on [the] function of that which is more modern in the evolution of the human animal. The psyche therefore has a fundamental unity with the body through its relation both to the function of tissue and organs and to the brain, as well as through the way it becomes intertwined with it by new relationships developed in the individual's fantasy or mind, conscious or unconscious.

THE SOUL For me the soul is a property of the psyche thus defined, and it too therefore depends eventually on brain function, and can be healthy or ill. I know that this is a personal view which is counter to the teaching of almost every religious system. It is with great diffidence therefore that I stick to the view I have formed. It is of great practical importance for every thinking person to come to a personal decision on this point, however, because of the modern treatment of mental disorder by leucotomy, that is by deliberate distortion of *healthy* brain functioning for the relief of suffering in the psyche.

For those who hold that the soul is implanted from without, and is not developed as a personal attribute, it is natural that there is no violation in leucotomy, which becomes then one of the many devices for the relief of suffering. For one who holds that the term "soul" (if it means anything at all) means something that grows in the individual, the deliberate distortion of *healthy* brain functioning is and must remain a price too big to pay for relief of suffering, since it alters irrevocably the basis for the existence of the psyche, soul included; and there is, after the treatment, no longer a whole person, psyche or soul, left.

According to my personal view it cannot be claimed that a patient is helped by leucotomy because of an observed relief from suffering. There may be a flaw in my argument, but the issues are so serious that those who use leucotomy as a therapy must be able to point to the flaw. It is not enough for them to continue to report removal of symptoms and the lessening of observed distress. There is no such thing as relief of suffering *in vacuo*; some person who suffers can be relieved; but it does not seem possible (to one holding my view on this point) to take responsibility for changing the person from one who suffers into quite something else, a part-human that does not suffer but which is not the original person who was brought for treatment.

It is for the purpose of keeping the relationship between the body and the psyche which is fundamental and which in health is established and maintained, that I use the term psyche–soma in the dissection of the personality. There is also the mind, a specialised part of the psyche that is not necessarily body-linked, though of course dependent on brain functioning. We indulge in a fantasy that there is a place, which we call the mind, where the intellect works, and each individual places the mind somewhere, and there feels muscular straining or experiences vascular congestion when trying to think. The brain itself is not used in the imagination for the placing of the mind, since there is no awareness of brain functioning; the brain functions silently and claims no acknowledgement.

EXCITED AND   In description of the healthy small child we
QUIET STATES   can usefully distinguish between the ex-
                       cited and the unexcited states. The in-
stincts clearly determine the problems of excited periods, and in the language of this chapter much that happens between excitement[s] is concerned either with warding off instinct, with preparing for eventual

satisfaction of instincts, or with keeping the instincts alive in an indirect way through play or the acting out of fantasy. In play the body comes into its own through the participation in acting out, and in fantasying, the body comes into its own in a secondary way through the fact that with fantasy there is appropriate localised somatic excitement, just as with body functioning there is fantasy. Masturbation of the ordinary healthy and relatively non-compulsive kind belongs to this keeping alive of the instincts in the absence of full-blown instinctual experience. In the case of children there is even more certainty of frustration in the instinct life than in the case of adults, and partly for this reason we see in childhood a relatively greater evaluation of play and of creative imagination.

In the first triangular relationship between persons which is being studied here, the child is overtaken by instinct and loves. This love involves physical and fantasy changes and is violent. It leads to hate. The child hates the third person. The child, having been an infant, already knows about love and aggression, and ambivalence and the fear that what is loved will be destroyed. Here at last, in the triangular relationship, hate can appear freely, since what is hated is a person, one who can defend himself, and one who is already loved; in fact (in the case of the boy) the father, the begetter, the mother's husband. Love of the mother is released, in the simplest case, by the father's becoming the hated object, the father who can survive and punish and forgive.

In health, at the height of excitement, anxiety is great and is tolerated as such. In this way recovery can take place, recovery from heightened instinct tension. It must always be true, however, that on account of painful conflict or because of fear, defences have to be organised, the neurotic child being not so much different from the normal healthy child as less conscious of what is going on and therefore more heavily and blindly defended against retribution.

THE OEDIPUS
COMPLEX

It is now possible to enumerate the various defences against anxiety which the child at this stage (who has come through infancy well) can adopt and organise. In the simplest possible case which Freud took for the development of his theory, the boy is in love with his mother. The father is used by the boy as a prototype of conscience. The boy takes in the father he knows and comes to terms with him. But other things happen and these can be enumerated. To some extent the boy loses instinct capacity, thus denying some of what he claimed. To some extent he displaces his love object, replaces mother by a sister, aunt, nurse, someone less involved with the father. To some extent the boy enters into a homosexual pact with the father, so that his potency becomes not entirely individual but instead (through identification) a new expression of the father's potency that has been taken in and adopted. All this is in the deep-seated dreams of the boy, and is not available for immediate conscious expression; but in health it is not absolutely unavailable. By identification with the father or father-figure the boy gets a potency by proxy, and a postponed potency of his own, which can be recovered at puberty.

The breakdown of defences appears as frank anxiety, either in the nightmare or in some manifestation during waking life. The nature of this manifestation depends not only on the physiology of fear,* but also on the nature of the fantasy, conscious or unconscious.

The healthy child who is negotiating all these hazards must be thought of as living in a relatively stable environment, with the mother happy in her marriage, and with the father ready to play his part with the children, to get to know his son and to give and take in the subtle way that comes fairly naturally to the father, who as a boy himself had a happy experience with his own father.

The tension rises as the child reaches to the height of early instinct functioning (somewhere between 2 and 5 years) and becomes then solved, or rather shelved, simply through the passage of time. As the latency period (as it is termed) arrives the child is released from having to adjust to developing instinct tension and is able to settle down for a few years, continuing in the inner world the experiences of what has been lived through and observed and imagined in the early phase of genital instinct dominance.

---

* Note that there is a physiology of fear, as of excitement or of hate, but there is no such thing as a physiology of anxiety, since manifestations of this complex state depend on the balance of fear, hate, love, excitement, etc., in the fantasy, and this is an affair of the individual.

Thus, by this way of looking at childhood, as by other methods, we see pain, suffering, and conflict, just as we see great joy.

RESTATEMENT   Freud had a way of describing these mat-
                                     ters which is now well known. He called the
                                     instinct drives the Id, and for the part of the
self that is in contact with the external world he used the word Ego. For many years his work was a study of the Ego's struggle with Id-impulses. This involved psychology in going to meet the Id in a way that had not been done before. By means of a technique for getting at the unconscious with the patient (psycho-analysis) Freud was able to show the world the nature and the strength of Id-impulses, that is to say, of instinct. He showed that what was associated with conflict and intolerable emotion became repressed, and a drain on the Ego's resources.

It was easy to say of psycho-analysis at that stage that it concerned itself only with the unpalatable, and it was quite usual for those who were hostile to this new investigation into human nature to assume that in psycho-analysis the Id and the unconscious were treated as one and the same thing. Yet what was being examined was the Ego's attempt to come to terms with the Id part of itself;* to become able to use Id-energy without too great a disturbance of the Ego's relation to the world or to the ideal.

Eventually (1923) Freud introduced the term Superego to describe at first the father taken in by the little boy and used for control of instinct. Freud knew that not quite the same could be said of little girls, but he allowed this theory to develop in his mind in this way, assuming that in time the matter would sort itself out; and I think it has. There remains a value in Freud's clear statement (much oversimplified as we know now) of the stages reached in health by the little boy who becomes able to set up in himself an ideal based on his idea of a real person, the actual father, a man that he knows well in real life, and with whom he can come to terms in his dream, or in his inner reality, or in deep fantasy. This is only possible when the child's development is continuing to go forward healthily and in a stable home environment.

---

* In psycho-analytic theory the Ego is thought of as a part of the Id.

By introducing the concept of the Superego Freud made it more clear than he had made it before in theoretical exposition that he was concerned with the Ego's problems, the growth of the Ego's conscience, the Ego-ideals and aims, and the Ego's defences against Id-drives. But this was always true in Freud's work; and it would have nullified the value of psycho-analysis if an earlier use of such a term as Superego had delayed the uncomfortable task of introducing the world's Ego to its Id.

The concept of the Superego has become widened in the course of time, although basically the term is used to describe whatever is built up or incorporated or organised within the Ego for control, direction, encouragement and support. Control is not only a direct control of instinct, but also a control of the complex phenomena of the Ego which depend on memories of instinctual experiences and their fantasy aspect. Consideration of this would take us, however, to the matter of a later section, namely that dealing with "the depressive position" in development.

In the language of this section the climax of emotional development is reached at the age of 3–4 years. The little boy or girl is fully established as a unit, able to feel that the persons around are whole persons too. In this setting the child is capable of genital sexual experience, except in so far as the physical procreativity of the human child is subject to postponement till puberty. In consequence of this endocrinological phenomenon of postponement, or what is called the latency period, the child must make the most of identification with the parents and other adults, and must make use of experience in dreams and play, of fantasying with or without bodily accompaniment, of bodily satisfactions obtained without other persons; the child must employ the pregenital or immature genital types of experience which are within the child's scope, and must make full use of the fact that the passage of time, a few hours or it may be minutes, brings relief from almost anything, however intolerable, provided someone who is understanding and familiar is present, keeping calm when hate, rage, anger, grief, despair, seem to be all.

Childhood sexuality is a very real thing; it can be immature or mature by the time the latency changes bring relief; and also, in so far as the quality of the child's sexuality is immature or distorted or inhibited at the end of this first period of interpersonal relationships, so will it reappear as immature or distorted or inhibited at puberty.

INFANTILE SEXUALITY   Freud saw that genital sexuality grew out of the pregenital and he called the instinctual life sexual except in so far as it was self-preservative. The term "infantile sexuality" therefore came into being, and many have wished Freud had not insisted on this part of his theory.

In my own personal opinion it was important for Freud to go to the full length of tracing the origins of adult or mature genital sexuality to childhood genital sexuality, and of showing the pregenital roots of childhood genitality. These pregenital instinctual experiences constitute infant sexuality. It is so easy to modify a concept to avoid giving offence, but a vitally important principle may be given away at the same time. Infant sexuality could have remained a term describing the compulsive genital exercises of certain infants who are deprived of loving care or seriously disturbed in their capacity for relationships. It has more value however as a description of the beginning of the whole development of instinct life. This is how Freud used the term. However, individual opinions on this matter of terminology will continue to be various.

It is possible as well as healthy for a child of 4 years to be at the stage of interpersonal relationships, with full employment of instincts, and with a full sexual life (except for the biological limitations described).

REALITY AND FANTASY   The healthy child becomes capable of the full dream of genital sexuality. In the remembered dream there can be found all the kinds of dream work that were carefully worked out by Freud. In the unremembered and unending dream the full consequences of the instinctual experience must be met. The boy who takes his father's place cannot avoid dealing with:

The idea of the death of the father and therefore of his own death.

The idea of castration by the father, or castration of the father.

The idea of being left with full responsibility for the satisfaction of the mother.

The idea of a compromise with the father, along homosexual lines.

In the girl's dream she cannot avoid dealing with:

The idea of the death of the mother and therefore of her own death.

The idea of robbing the mother of her husband, of his penis, of her children, and so the idea of her own sterility.

The idea of being at the mercy of the father's sexuality.

The idea of a compromise with the mother along homosexual lines.

When parents actually exist, and also a home setting and the continuance of familiar things, the solution comes through the sorting out of what is called reality and fantasy. Seeing the parents together makes the dream of their separation, or of the death of one of them, tolerable. The primal scene (parents together sexually) is the basis of individual stability since it makes possible the whole dream of taking the place of one partner. This does not discount the fact that the primal scene, the actual witnessing of intercourse, can put the maximum strain on a child and can (by happening quite apart from the child's needs) be traumatic, so that as a result of being forced to witness it a child starts to develop illness. Both statements are needed, showing the value and also the danger of the primal scene.

Parents who are otherwise satisfactory may easily fail in child care by being unable to distinguish clearly between the child's dream and fact. They may present an idea as a fact, or thoughtlessly react to an idea as if it had been an action. They may indeed be more frightened of ideas than of actions. Maturity means, among other things, a capacity for tolerating ideas, and parents need this capacity which at its best is part of a social maturity. A mature social system (while making certain demands in regard to action) allows freedom of ideas and the free expression of them.* The child only gradually reaches the ability to distinguish between dream and reality.

The healthy child to some extent fails to tolerate the conflicts and anxieties that reach their climax at the climax of instinctual experience. A solution of childhood's inherent problems of ambivalence comes through the imaginative elaboration of all function; without fantasy crude expression of appetite and of sexuality and of hate would be the rule. Fantasy in this way proves to be the human characteristic, the stuff of socialisation and of civilisation itself.

THE UNCONSCIOUS   The essential idea in all this description of the healthy and the neurotic (not psychotic) child is that of the unconscious and the special examples of unconscious known as "the repressed unconscious".

The main work of psycho-analytic treatment concerns psycho-neurotic patients, and comes about through bringing to consciousness that which was unconscious. This is chiefly done through the reliving in the relationship of the patient to the analyst. The psycho-neurotic appears to work from consciousness, and feels uncomfortable about that which is unavailable to consciousness. A desire for self-awareness seems to be characteristic of the psycho-neurotic. Analysis, for these people, brings increased awareness and tolerance of unawareness. In contrast to this, the psychotic (and normal people of psychotic type) are not very much concerned with awareness, and exist in feeling and in mystic experience, even suspecting or despising intellectual awareness. The latter do not expect to become more aware, through analysis, but they do gradually come to hope to be enabled to feel real.

In psycho-analytic work the analyst is regularly presented with striking proof of the unconscious when the patient unexpectedly brings into the analytic situation that which was previously unconscious, even strongly denied. In the relationship between the psycho-

---

* See: Winnicott, D.W.: (1950) "Some Thoughts on the Meaning of the Word 'Democracy'" and Money-Kyrle, R.E.: (1951) *Psycho-Analysis and Politics*.

neurotic patient and the analyst there appears and reappears a specialised relationship which bears the stamp of the patient's neurosis, and which is the illness of the patient appearing in samples. This phenomenon is called the "transference neurosis". The result of analysis of the transference neurosis is the appearance of the illness bit by bit in the highly specialised and controlled conditions which the analyst undertakes, provides, and maintains.

The unpardonable sin in psycho-therapy would be the analyst's use of the analytic relationship for personal gratification. This principle is very near that underlying the original oath of doctors, which proscribes sexual intercourse with a patient; thus Hippocrates showed that he understood in the year [400] B.C. that there is value in allowing the patient to bring to the professional relationship patterns that are personal and, as we would say, derived from the Oedipus Complex and the inverted Oedipus Complex and set originally in early childhood. What Freud did in addition was to use the patient's personal contribution to the professional relationship in an ordered attempt to bring the past into the present, and so to give conditions in which change and growth can occur where otherwise there is rigidity.

The abuse of the transference neurosis would be like the sexual seduction of a small child, since the small child is not able to make true object choice, being not yet free from a high degree of subjectivity in observation. A corollary of this is that it is very difficult for a patient who has been seduced in childhood to believe in and to trust an analyst exactly at the point at which the analyst can most effectually operate. It can be noted here that the analysis of psychosis of schizoid type* is essentially different from the analysis of psycho-neurosis, because the former requires of the analyst a toleration of actual regression to dependence, while the latter needs something different, an ability to tolerate ideas and feelings (love, hate, ambivalence, etc.) and an understanding of processes, and also a wish to show understanding by appropriate exposition in language (interpretation of what the patient is just ready to allow to consciousness). A correct and well-timed interpretation in an analytic treatment gives a sense of being held

---

* Psychosis of manic-depressive type is not being referred to at this point.

physically that is more real (to the non-psychotic) than if a real holding or nursing had taken place. Understanding goes deeper and by understanding, shown by the use of language, the analyst holds physically in the past, that is, at the time of the need to be held, when love meant physical care and adaptation.

SUMMARY

There is thus, in health, a maturity of instinct development that is reached at roughly 5 years, that is to say, before the biological fact of latency. At puberty the patterns of instinct development and the organisations of defence against anxiety which were present in the pre-latency era reappear and largely determine the instinct pattern and capacity of the adult. If organised defences against anxiety are more in evidence than the instincts and their conscious control and their influence on action and imagination, then the clinical picture is of psycho-neurosis rather than of health.

Growth takes place as long as a person is alive, especially if the person is healthy, but in the matter of the quality of instincts, their availability and their control and their neurotic limitation, there is relatively little growth after the tremendous forward movement that is crowded into the early years when (ordinarily) the family provides the ideal setting for such growth. This is true in spite of the fact of the great changes belonging to the age of puberty, changes which have endocrinological backing, changes which make procreation a part of actual genital function for the first time in the individual's life.

These matters, which concern the analyst in his hour by hour work with the psycho-neurotically ill, are important for the student of human nature. It is true, however, that for those who are not learning to become analysts (the majority of my readers) the phenomena of instinct development and the defences against castration anxiety are not of much practical concern. If a child has a phobia it is of limited practical value for a teacher to be told what would be found *if the child were to have an analysis*, especially as analysis is very seldom available.

Nevertheless, it is useful for anyone trusted with the care of children to have what understanding is available, and in the management of small children it is certainly a help if something is known of the reasons why a stable setting is essential. Tremendous forces are at work derived from instincts, and in the years 2–5 each child has to come to terms with heredity, instincts, body peculiarities, environmental factors both good and bad, while at the same time building up personal relationships, likes and dislikes, a personal conscience, and hopes for the future.

Chart Showing Psychology of Small Boy in Terms of Instinct Theory

Love of mother

Hate of father   Kill or die

Neither kill   Time factor   Castrate or
nor die   fantasy*   be castrated

Castration
anxiety
(intolerable)

Defences Against Anxiety – Castration Threat

Inhibition of instinct (source of love)

Object abandoned, substitute accepted.

Identification with rival, loss of personal identity.

Homosexual compromise with rival
(passive)

Instinct regression to pregenital
(love maintained, but castration threat avoided,
use of bad fixation points)

Regression to dependence
(love maintained, maturation abandoned,
use of good fixation points)

---

* *Note for revision:* Develop to survival of object; origin of fantasy as in "Use of Object" paper.

Guilt acknowledged, expiation organised (obsessional),
    (hence crime permitted).

Repression of part of the love (or hate)
    (unawareness maintained)
    cost: energy expended and loss of capacity to love
    (or hate)

In health the child is able to employ any or all of these (and other) defences against anxiety. Anxiety is not the abnormality so much as the child's inability to employ some defences or a special liability to employ one type of defence.

BREAKDOWN OF DEFENCES

Anxiety:	nightmare or anxiety attack
new defences:	exploitation of somatic manifestations of anxiety with secondary gain (cf. regression to dependence)
	anaesthesia in place of repression loss of pleasure in physical climax
Confusion:	general confusion between anxiety and excitement
new defences:	order, designed to hide confusion (obsessional)
Return of the repressed:	the love (or hate) appears, temporarily, but is not fully acknowledged.
new defences:	deeper repression at greater cost.

And so on.

PART III

ESTABLISHMENT OF UNIT STATUS

Introduction:
Emotional development
characteristic of infancy

In the foregoing section the instincts and the progression of types of instinct dominance determined the method of study of human nature. Much of what now follows concerns the child before the age of genital dominance. The study of interpersonal relationships has acquired a language of its own, with a set of terms from the early work of Freud and now integrated into common usage.

In this section dealing with emotional development that is characteristic of infancy a different descriptive method will be used. It will not be assumed that the child has become able to manage a triangular relationship, but the subject of study will be the infant's capacity for forming a relationship with one other (the mother). Once again it is necessary to take for granted healthy development at yet earlier stages, those that will be examined in Part IV. Some things will be accounted for that have been missing hitherto, for instance the idea of *value* in the child who is developing. The idea of value cuts right across the idea of health but the two are not unrelated. Value may increase at any age, or may diminish; it may also be hidden and become unavailable, thus reminding one of instinct that is inhibited and of fantasy that is repressed.

I am describing the stage of development at which an infant becomes a unit, becomes able to feel the self (and therefore others) to be whole, a one thing with a limiting membrane, and with an inside and an outside. This, as I have said, assumes the whole of the development that leads up to this sense of being one.

The concepts of the previous section were intellectual concepts in the mind of the observer. I adopted the concepts of consciousness and of the unconscious, and of the repressed unconscious. Now, instead, it is more profitable to use a diagram which could be a child's drawing. Let us say that a child has been covering paper with lines and to–fro movements, and has been wandering round with the pencil going from place to place, occasionally slipping incontinently over the edge; and then something new turns up, a line that joins up with its beginning, a rough circle is made, and the child points and says: "duck" or even "Tommy" or "Anne". The diagram we need, in fact, is the child's conception of the self, a sphere, which is a circle in a two-dimensional drawing.

The infant comes gradually up to the position that I am now examining. Characteristically at this stage there is a progress of the following kind:

The idea of a limiting membrane appears, and from this follows the idea of an inside and an outside. Then there develops the theme of a ME and a not-ME. There are now ME contents that depend partly on instinctual experience. There follows the possibility of a feeling of responsibility for instinctual experience, and for ME contents, and a feeling of independence of what is outside. A meaning comes to the term "relationship" as between the person, ME, and objects. The result of this is a recognition of something equivalent to ME in mother, that is to say the feeling of her as a person, the breast being then a part of a person.

CHAPTER I

THE DEPRESSIVE POSITION

CONCERN, GUILT AND
INNER PERSONAL
PSYCHIC REALITY

ALONG WITH ALL THIS goes a sorting out of the two states, the quiet and the excited. Ruthlessness in the instinctual "attack" on the object gives way to a dawning appreciation of the mother as a person caring for the ME and at the same time a person presenting the part of herself for the feed. There gradually comes about an integrating of excited and quiet types of relationship, and a recognition of the fact that the two states together (not one only) constitute a total relationship with [the] mother-person. Here is what is called "The Depressive Position in Emotional Development", an important stage which involves the infant in guilt feelings, and concern about relationships on account of their instinctual or excited elements.

The child's anxieties are of a highly complex order. There is a concern not only about the effect on the person of the mother because of instinctual elements in the relationship between the ME and herself, two persons, (guilt); but also concern on account of the changes within that follow excited experiences, and experiences tinged with anger or actuated by hate (hypochondriacal anxiety). (Added to these are the anxieties called paranoid, which will be examined separately.)

It can easily be seen that there is a tremendous amount of growth in this progression from ruthlessness to concern, from ME-dependence to ME-relationships, from preambivalence to ambivalence, from a primary dissociation between quiet and excited states to an integration of these two aspects of the self.

The infant is engaged in a task which absolutely needs both *time* and a continuing *personal environment*. The mother-person holds the situation in time while the infant finds a way to reach "the depressive position", and without her continued personal care this development cannot take place. Resolution occurs in the following way.

It may be taken as axiomatic that the human infant is not able to bear the burden of guilt and fear that belongs to a full recognition of the fact that the aggressive ideas in primitive ruthless instinctual love are directed towards the mother of the dependent (anaclitic) relationship. Moreover the child is not yet advanced enough to make use of the idea of a father intervening, and by intervening making the instinctual ideas safe. Resolution of the difficulty which is inherent in life at this stage comes through a capacity that the infant develops for making reparation. If the mother holds the situation, day by day, then the infant has time to sort out the rich imaginative results of instinctual experience, and to rescue something that is felt to be "good", supportive, acceptable, unhurting, and with this imaginatively to repair the damage done to the mother. Over and over again in the ordinary infant–mother relationship this hurting-made-good takes place, and gradually the infant comes to believe in constructive effort, and to be able to bear guilt and so to be free to love instinctually.

In this way the healthy infant is at first, with the mother accepting a high degree of dependence as natural, independent of the father who is otherwise absolutely needed to protect the mother, unless the infant is to become inhibited, to lose the capacity for excited love. The gain is seen clinically in the healthy child's capacity to be in a depressed mood, to be holding guilt-feelings until such time as a working-through of recent events and their imaginative elaboration in the unconscious have produced the material for something constructive either in relationships or in play or in work.

It is presumably because the depression mood comes in here clinically that the term "depressive position in normal emotional development" was employed. This does not mean that the normal infant goes through a depressive or mood *illness*. A depressive illness in an infant* is indeed an abnormal state, and one that is not met with in

---

* See Spitz, R.A. [(1945): "Hospitalism"].

the case of the normal infant in ordinary good personal care. Under suitable conditions, then, the infant becomes able to sort out the good and the bad within the self.* A highly complex inner state arises, samples of which appear in play and especially in the treatment room in the course of psycho-therapy. In psycho-therapy (the infant being now a small child) the room often stands for the child's limited psyche, and the analyst is allowed in this way into the child's inner world, where there is a tremendous contention between forces, where magic controls, and where the good is constantly in danger from the bad. It feels mad to be in the child's inner world. From what obtains in the child's inner world that we can be shown we can deduce the elements of the inner world of infants.

The bad is held a little, for use in the expression of anger, and the good is held for personal growth and for reparation and restitution, for making good where damage has been imaginatively done.

I am referring chiefly, of course, to the infant's unconscious feelings and ideas, to the content of the psyche that exists apart from the child's intellectual efforts at understanding.

With the mother (or mother-substitute) still present and available, that is to say with the infant in an environment suitable for an infant, there gradually comes about a moment of mending, a moment in which the infant uses the capacity that has developed in the previous hours of contemplation or digestion. Perhaps the infant actually does something (smiles or makes a spontaneous gesture of love, or offers a gift – an excretion product – as a token of reparation and restitution).

---

* The words good and bad are an inheritance from the dim past; they are also suitable words for description of the extremes that every infant feels about inside matters – whether these be forces, objects, sounds or smells. I am not referring here to the use of the terms good or bad by parents and nurses who wish to implant morality on the infant.

Everything in this section comes from my own work. Much is based on what I have gathered from the teachings and writings of Melanie Klein, and from personal tuition from her. In many respects my way of putting things is not hers, and I know that she disagrees with certain details of my presentation. I have not attempted, however, to give her exact views as they have been fully stated by herself and by Isaacs, Heimann, Segal and others. My chief wish here is to make full acknowledgement.

The breast (body, mother) is now mended, and the day's work is done. Tomorrow's instincts can be awaited with limited fear. Sufficient unto the day is the evil thereof.

In the depressed mood, it could be said that the infant (or child or adult) blankets the total inner situation, or lets a control descend over it, a fog, or mist, or a kind of paralysis. This makes possible a gradual lifting (in the course of time) of the magical controls, so that sorting can be carried out bit by bit, till eventually it is possible for the mood to lift, and for the child's inner world to come alive again.

There are other kinds of depression, those of schizoid persons. These are related to depersonalisation rather than to the more normal mechanism of magical control with healing purpose. The depression mood I am describing is related closely to normal mourning, and to the whole subject of reaction to loss.* At the start, in infancy, weaning is something that becomes meaningful after (and not before) the infant has reached the depressive position.

As a result of the success of reparative action and ideas, the infant becomes bolder to allow new instinct experience; inhibition is lessened, and this leads to richer results from instinctual experience. There is thus a bigger task in the next digestive or contemplative phase, but with good the fortune of continued and personal mother-care there comes a bigger capacity for mending, and so there follows a new degree of freedom of instinct experience. In fact a benign circle is set up which forms the basis for infant life over a considerable period.

It will easily be appreciated how important, at this stage, is the continuity of relationship between the baby and the actual mother (or substitute mother). In an institution, where the "mother" who feeds in the morning is not the "mother" who baths and manages in the evening, the infant's day by day capacity for making reparation is wasted, and the benign circle is not established. Worse still, where feeding is itself impersonal and mechanical (and this can happen in the actual home of a child) there is no room for the development that is being described here.

---

* This part of psycho-analytic theory was developed from Freud's *Mourning and Melancholia*.

DIAGRAM I

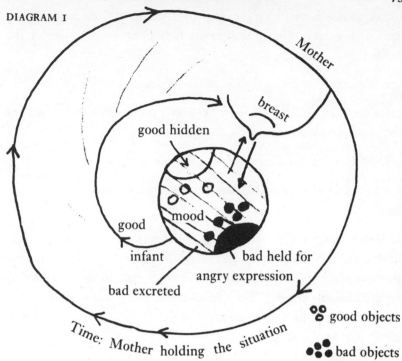

good hidden

breast

Mother

mood

good

infant

bad held for
angry expression

bad excreted

Time: Mother holding the situation

good objects

bad objects

The development of the capacity for concern is therefore a complex affair, and it depends on a continuing personal relationship between an infant and a mother-figure.

The noteworthy feature of this theory of the benign circle at the depressive position is that it accounts for the fact that in health a fairly full recognition of the aggressive and destructive factors in instinct love and its fantasy is possible for the developing individual. It should be remembered that in infancy there is a very limited capacity for actual reparation apart from the mother's ready acceptance of the token gift, as compared with the adult's capacity for social contribution through work. At the same time the infant's destructive and aggressive impulses are no less than that of the adult. From this it could be deduced, if it were not already known, that the infant is more dependent on the love that others bestow than are adults, so that a smile or tiny gesture has an effect equivalent to an adult's day's work.

To repeat what has been said, it is not possible for a human being to stand the destructiveness that is basic in human relationships, that is

to say, in instinctual loving, except by a gradual development associated with the experience of reparation and restitution. If there is a
break in the benign circle, then

(1) instinct (or capacity for loving) must become inhibited

(2) a dissociation must reappear between the infant who is excited and
the same person when quiet

(3) the sense of quiet is no longer available, and

(4) the capacity for constructive play (and work equivalent) becomes
lost.

In fact, potency and the acceptance of potency are not to be described
in terms of instinct development alone. In a theoretical description of
the development of sexual capacity it is insufficient to speak in terms of
progression of instinct dominance alone, since hope in regard to
recovery from guilt over destructive ideas is a vitally important
element in potency.*

The nature of the destructive impulses and ideas will be discussed
later. The primitive love impulse is perhaps destructive in aim, or the
destructiveness comes about from the inevitable frustrations that
interfere with immediate satisfaction (see pp.79,131–4).

The so-called "depressive position" is by no means a matter that
affects only the theoretician and the psycho-therapist. Parents and
teachers are very much concerned with this process of the establishment of the benign circle. It is true that this process starts when the
infant is only a few months old and it is then the mother who holds the
original situation, doing it well and naturally, while scarcely knowing
what she is doing. But this vital mechanism of growth continues, and
the teacher who provides the child with the tools and techniques for
constructive play and work and who supplies a goal for effort through
personal appreciation is in the same position of importance, or necessity, as the minder of an infant. The infant-minder, and the teacher
scarcely less, is available to receive the infant's spontaneous gesture of

---

* See Klein [1932, 1934] also Henderson, D.K. and Gillespie, R.D.: [1940]: potency
in abeyance by depressed mood.

love which neutralises the infant's concern, remorse, guilt, belonging to the ideas that had turned up at the height of instinctual experience.* (This will be re-examined in the study of environmental influences, pp.152 ff.)

Important new ways of pursuing the description of human nature follow the acceptance of the depressive position (by whatever name it be called) in the theoretical construct.

The infant's inside or inner world or inner reality is built up of three elements:

(1) The instinctual experiences themselves
    a. satisfactory   good
    b. unsatisfactory, complicated by
    anger at frustration   bad

(2) Objects incorporated (instinctual experience)
    a. in love   good
    b. in hate   bad

(3) Objects or experiences taken in magically
    a. for control   bad potential
    b. for use in enrichment or for control   good potential

No chart is satisfactory except temporarily to the person making it and each reader who is inclined to do so will naturally make a chart that is specially descriptive of his or her own peculiar slant on whatever is being discussed.

There are charts that I find useful in practical work (Diagram 2).

It will be noted that the result of functional incorporation of "good breasts" is a general, non-specific increase of goodness inside. On the other hand introjected (recognisable) "good breasts" are evidence of a previous idealisation, and introjection is magical, not part of instinctual experience. There is an important lesson for the teacher

---

* It is only fair to certain psycho-analysts to say that many are not in favour of the use of the concept of the depressive position. It is well known that one leading analyst (Edward Glover) feels so strongly that the idea of the depressive position represents a false step that he has resigned from the British Psycho-Analytical Society, although he has retained personal membership of the International Psycho-Analytical Society.

DIAGRAM 2

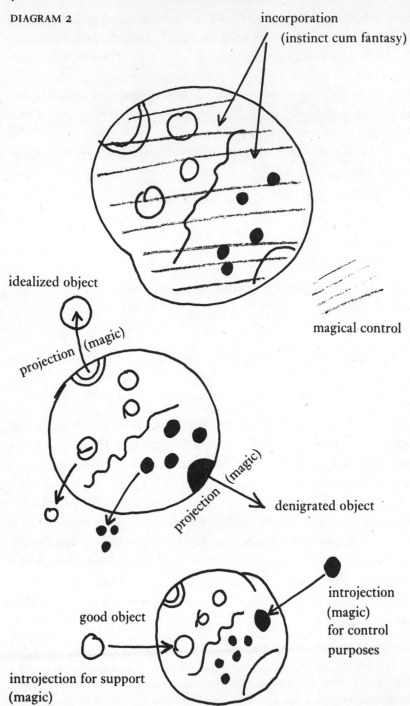

incorporation
(instinct cum fantasy)

idealized object

projection (magic)

magical control

projection (magic)

denigrated object

projection (magic)

good object

introjection
(magic)
for control
purposes

introjection for support
(magic)

here, since in her most successful work she will not be recognisable in her pupils – who will, so to speak, have incorporated her and her lessons, and will have grown on them. By contrast, there will be some magical introjection of her and her teachings after idealisation, and this may seem rather nice, but the disadvantage is that the pupils have not grown in the true sense of the word. Ordinarily in a class there is a happy admixture of these two kinds of teaching and learning.

During the period of contemplation (after a feed) there is a holding up of instinct and a need for external control of environmental impingement. The in-turning of the hypochondriacal phase produces vulnerability, and this means that for the phase to be possible there must be good enough management.

Tremendous forces are at work within the person when, as in health, they have full vitality. To get a glimpse into the task of sorting out after instinctual experience we must refer to the work of artists who (because of their exceptional technique and confidence in their work) become able to risk nearly the full force of what is there in human nature. A late Beethoven string quartet, Blake's illustrations for Job, a Dostoevsky novel, a political history of England, these show us something of the complexity of the inner world, the interweaving of good and bad, the reservation of the good, the control yet the full acknowledgement of the bad. These things start in full force in the infant's inner world (located by the infant in the belly) though of course it is true that in the course of time, as experience of life becomes more rich, the inner world becomes more and more rich in content. The basic forces and the strife are present from the beginning, however, as soon as instinctual experiences are the lot of the infant.

Gradually, out of the inner world there is produced some sort of pattern, order out of chaos. This labour is not mental or intellectual, but a task of the psyche. It is closely related to the task of digestion, a task that is also performed apart from intellectual understanding. Intellectual understanding may or may not follow.

The infant who has achieved a stability at this stage is now able to get rid of this, keep that, give this in love and give that in hate. Also because of the internal sorting processes there can be allowed a kind of going on living, but a living that is within the psyche (imagined to be

within the belly). From this time forward growth is not only of the
body and of the self in relation to objects both outside and in; it is also a
growth going on in the inside, like a novel being all the time written, a
world developing within the child. In health there is plenty of opportunity for interchange between this life in the inner world and the
external world of living and of relationships. Each enriches the other.
(What happens in ill-health will be described later. See pp.81 ff and
pp.94 ff.)

THE DEPRESSIVE   A. All previous development being taken
POSITION: for granted:
RECAPITULATION
                        B. The infant or child begins, at times, to
                        feel the self to be of limited dimensions:

C. The self becomes more and more firmly felt as a unit:

D. An object external to the self is felt to be a whole thing:

E. This feeling of the wholeness of the self refers at the same time to
body and to psyche, so that in a child's drawing of a circle as a
self-portrait there is no differentiation between body and psyche:

(I assume all the time a mother-person holding the situation, day
by day, week in, week out).

F. Add to this wholeness of spatial type a similar tendency for a
coming together of the self in time, a joining up of past, present and
future:

G. The stage is now set for a relationship that has new features, new in
that the infant or child has become able to have experiences and to be
altered by them while yet retaining personal integrity, individuality,
being.

H. Excited phases in relationships, with instincts involved, test the
newly developed structure, and especially when the infant who is in a
quiet state between excitements contemplates the results of excited
action and idea.

I. The infant becomes *concerned*, and in two ways:

1. Concern about the object of excited loving.
2. Concern about the results in the self of excited experience.
These two are inter-related, because it is only in so far as the infant is becoming able to develop a structural self, with an inside richness, that the loved object is also felt to be a structured and valuable person.

J. Concern for the loved object arises on account of aggressive, destructive, acquisitive elements in the primitive love impulse which is gradually becoming assimilated to the whole self (joining up of the personality in time). The child now is becoming responsible for what happened at the last meal and what will happen at the next.

The primitive impulse was ruthless, from the point of view of the observer. For the infant the primitive impulse is pre-ruth, and only becomes felt as having been ruthless as the child integrates finally to one responsible person and looks back. From the achievement of integration (but not earlier) the child controls the instinctual impulses on account of the threatened ruthlessness, which engenders intolerable guilt – that is to say, recognition of the destructive element in the crude primitive excited idea.*

Guilt about the primitive love impulses is an achievement of development; it is too great for the human infant to bear, except by a gradual process following the setting up of the benign circle which has been described. Even so the primitive love impulse continues to provide the basis for the difficulties inherent in life, that is to say, difficulties that belong to the healthy, and more to the healthy than to

---

* It is thought by many that the primary excited impulse is not destructive, but that the destructiveness enters into the imaginative elaboration through anger at frustration. Part and parcel of this theory, however, is that of the omnipotence of the infant, so that the result is the same. The infant becomes angry since adaptation to need is never complete. Nevertheless I consider personally that this theory, although it is correct, is not basic, since this anger at frustration does not go early enough. At the present time I find I need to assume that there is a primary aggressive and destructive impulse that is indistinguishable from instinctual love appropriate to the very early stage of development of the infant.

[Added] 1970. N.B. This is the reason why I could not publish this book. The matter resolved itself, for me, in "The Use of an Object" [in Winnicott, D.W: *Playing and Reality*].

those who have not been able to reach "the depressive position" in development, that specific which enables the full experience of concern. Psychotics, those with disturbances derived from a still earlier and more basic level, these have their difficulties and their problems, and these are especially irksome because of their being not inherent, not so much a part of life as a part of the struggle to reach a life – successful treatment of a psychotic enables the patient to *begin* to live and to begin to experience the inherent difficulties of life.

Probably the greatest suffering in the human world is the suffering of normal or healthy or mature persons. This is not generally recognised. It is surely a false guide to observe manifest perplexity, misery and pain in a mental hospital. Nevertheless it is usual for degree of suffering to be assessed in this superficial way.

K. Concern over the results in the self of instinctual experiences.

REPRESSION RECONSIDERED   The concept of repression that is essential in the theory of human nature formulated according to progression of instinct dominance becomes now something that we can illustrate by using the infant's own imagination. We can say that certain incorporated objects, or relationships between objects, or certain introjected experiences become (as it were) *encysted*, surrounded by powerful defence forces which keep them from becoming assimilated, or from gaining a free life in amongst all the rest of that which is inside.

The infant or child is not ever free from doubt about the self, since this task of sorting and redistribution is never complete, and whatever is complete is disturbed by the next instinctual experience.

Thus there is an enrichment of the fantasy from each new experience and a strengthening of the feeling of the reality of the experience. When the body is involved in experiences we use terms like incorporation, and excretion or evacuation, terms that allow for a body function and psyche elaboration. When danger from the internal situation is great, there can be no waiting for opportunities afforded by external reality for instinctual or functional expression, and then the more magical processes have to be employed for which we use the terms "introjection" and "projection".

THE MANAGEMENT
OF BAD FORCES
AND OBJECTS

The bad internal phenomenon that cannot be countered or controlled or ousted becomes a nuisance. It becomes a persecutor within and is felt by the child as a threat from within. Very easily this becomes a pain. A pain due to physical disease is perhaps invested with the properties called persecutory. Severe pain can be tolerated when separated from the idea of the bad internal object or force, and, on the other hand, where there is a state of expected persecution from within quite small disorders or bodily sensations can be felt as pain; in other words there is brought about a lowered threshold of tolerance of pain.

The persecuting elements may become intolerable and they are then projected, found in the external world. Either there is some capacity for toleration, in which case the child waits for a situation in which there is some real persecution from outside and then feels this in an exaggerated way, or else there is no toleration and the child hallucinates a bad or persecutory object; that is to say, a persecutor is magically projected, and is found outside the self delusively. Thus, when there is expectation of persecution, actual persecution produces relief, this relief being due to the fact that the individual need not feel deluded or mad.

Clinically it is common to find two states alternating, namely: internal persecution (some intolerable condition with or without basis in body disease process) and delusion of external persecution with temporary relief from the inner or physical complaint.

There is a clinical state in which a child is, so to speak, halfway between being unable and able to manage to get rid of bad objects by excretion, being too much in fear of the persecutory element in the faeces to complete the process. The presenting symptom is usually constipation, with the faeces (that are hardening by being dehydrated while held in the rectum) representing the persecutor. It was not known at the time that this theory was first put forward* that the persecutor began to persecute when in the belly, and in fact derived its persecutory quality from the oral sadistic impulse.

It often happens that parents (and doctors and nurses) have a fear

---

* [Ophuijsen, J.H.W. van: (1920) "On the Origin of the Feeling of Persecution".]

of faeces. This fear displays itself in a persistent clearing out of the children's rectums, either by aperient or by washout or suppository. A child so treated is left no opportunity for coming to terms with the persecuting ideas in a natural way. Also, the parents' action leads easily to anal over-stimulation; thus the anus becomes over-emphasised as an erotic organ, and takes over erotism that belongs to the mouth. The anus under these circumstances may become more important to the owner as an excitable receptive organ than as a passer-on and passer-out of material no longer useful, and potentially persecutory.

The child's well-known interest in faeces, and so of substitutes for faeces, and in the fate of the faeces and in drainage systems generally, derives force from the potential persecutor quality in faeces. The equivalent of this can be expressed in terms of urinary function.

Eventually, when full genital function is established, the semen may become equated with potential persecution; if so, it must be got rid of or it will damage the body inside. Then the semen is bad and cannot possibly feel to the man to be able to bring about conception of a child in a loved woman (even when in actual fact it has, and the healthy child that has resulted is there before the eyes of the man). A lesser degree of this explains the healthy man's concern for the woman he has impregnated, in other words, his sense of paternity.

In the woman the equivalent of this is a feeling that a man could have nothing to offer but persecuting elements that he is afraid of, and she can only try to avoid being used in a man's effort to have bad stuff taken off his hands. In this way residues of inner conflicts unresolved can interfere with sexual capacity.

INNER RICHNESS
AND COMPLEXITY

The inner world can now be seen as something that can become infinitely rich, but not perhaps infinitely complex; the complexity is something that grows naturally, and that has a simple foundation.

Interesting light is thrown on the workings of the inner world and of the individual's relation to it by examination of the ways the inner world is affected by psycho-therapy of one kind and another.

The "depressive position" is of interest to all who are concerned with human beings of whatever age. These matters of very early emotional development too are not just phenomena of theoretical interest; they are matters which are and which go on being the basic task of every human being throughout life. The tasks remain the same, but as the [human] being grows and develops there is more of the individual there, engaged in the real struggle that is life.*†

* [At this point a note was left in the typescript:]
  Weaning Include here paper on weaning
[It is likely that the note referred to the chapter on "Weaning" (1949) now in Winnicott, D.W.: *The Child, the Family and the Outside World*.]

† [A note in the margin alongside this paragraph said "re-write".]

CHAPTER 2

DEVELOPMENT OF THE THEME
OF THE INNER WORLD

INTRODUCTION   I N T H I S D E S C R I P T I O N the inner world is the personal world in so far as it is, in fantasy, held within the bounds of the Ego – and within the body's skin. This inner world can now be examined as a thing in itself, though of course in life the inner world of a person is all the time subject to changes according to the events in the external relationships of that person, and according to the instinctual impulses that reach climax, or that only partially succeed, or that quite fail to reach gratification.

The inner world comes to have a stability of its own, but changes in it are related to the experiences of the whole self in external relationships. Unsatisfactory* experiences lead to the existence and the strengthening of things or forces felt to be bad within. These until bound, or controlled or eliminated, are internal persecutors. The child knows of their existence and threat by a sense of pain or illness, or lowered threshold of sensitivity to sensory discomfort.

PARANOID   Groupings of persecutors that constitute
WAY OF LIFE   too big a threat and that cannot wait for excretion (linked to instinctual experience) must be eliminated by projection, that is, magically. If there is something that can be perceived to be bad in the immediate external world this becomes the persecutor and the child's paranoid system is hidden in the reaction to the external real threat. If nothing bad is

---

* The meaning of "unsatisfactory" here will be discussed later (see pages 107 ff and 126 ff).

available then the child must hallucinate a persecutory element and a delusion of persecution results. Individuals gradually learn how to get the world to persecute them, so that they may get the relief from internal persecution without the madness of the delusion.

It is interesting to see how early the paranoid way of life can show clinically. The condition of expected persecution may develop after a child has had some years of life with no obvious persecutory tendency; in such a case, however, there is some big trauma to account for the change – concussion – mastoid operation – a chance coincidence of two or three adverse factors. It is often possible, however, to make the diagnosis with confidence in infancy.

A point of onset is usually clear in the history, but the sensitivity to persecution, suspicion and unfriendliness is not rarely present from the very beginning when the mother failed (perhaps through no fault of her own) in her first establishment of a relationship, and in her first efforts to present the world to the infant.*

Many infants who have what looks like a hypersensitive disposition are brought through to some confidence in the world by prolonged and exceptionally adaptive nursing care; and it is often possible even with older children with a persecution expectation to bring about an amelioration of the condition by specialised management.

In psycho-therapy the necessary deep changes come through the releasing of oral sadism from repression; this can only be done in an intensive personal analytic treatment.

DEPRESSION AND THE   Depression as a mood has many causes:
"DEPRESSIVE POSITION"
                           (1) Loss of vitality due to control of
                               instinct at the first moments of coming
together from a dissociated state into wholeness.

(2) Ordinary healthy doubt, the state of self-realisation that follows instinctual experience, before a period of time and contemplation has made possible the sorting out of good and bad and the temporary pattern of management of inner objects and forces and phenomena.

---

* See later, pp. 107 ff and 126 ff.

(3) Depression that appears as a mood when doubt about inner phenomena is too great, so that a blind damping down of the whole life of the inner world is adopted as a defence. This is an exaggeration of (2), amounting to a pathological state.

It is to be noted that there are other extremely important meanings for the clinical term depression, and the concept of [the] so-called "depressive position" as a stage in normal development is not helpful in the elucidation of (for instance) the depression that belongs to depersonalisation.

Depression in infancy is a clinical phenomenon that has been well described and [is] not uncommon; there are, however, some rather rare physical conditions that have to be remembered in differential diagnosis (Pink's Disease,* for instance).

Klein (according to my view) has not stated that infants normally become depressed, that is, get into a clinical state of depressed mood, although she knows that in illness they may do so. She has claimed, however, that the capacity to become depressed, to have a reactive depression, to mourn loss, is something that is not inborn, nor is it an illness; it comes as an achievement of healthy emotional growth, and there is a time in the development of every healthy infant at which it can be said that this capacity has now arrived. The name "depressive position in emotional development" has been given to this stage of development, and if a better name can be found it can be used. The important thing is the infant's or the individual's new capacity to accept responsibility for the destructive aim in the total love impulse, including the anger at the frustration which is inevitable because of the omnipotence in the infant's claims.

THE MANIC DEFENCE   Essential to healthy development is a certain seriousness, a doubt about the self, a need for periods of contemplation, and liability to temporary phases of hopelessness. These conditions can become transformed temporarily into a kind of opposite, like a holiday which is the opposite to work.

In health depression is potential and at the core of the personality,

---

* [Lead poisoning.]

and is evidence of health. This depression makes itself manifest in a certain capacity for seriousness, and also in doubts which may easily take the form of vague physical ill-health. It also shows in the form of denied depression, which is hidden in the happiness and the restless activity and general liveliness which are associated in our minds with the idea of early childhood. Thus normally, in the total life of a child, the manic-depressive swing appears in the to and fro of childhood liveliness punctuated by moments of acute misery, or frustration interrupted by phases of acute joy.

The depressed mood scarcely appears as such except in the special case of the deprived child. Ordinarily depression hides under some kind of unwellness which is met by the mother's solicitude. Denial of depression hides in the exaggeration of the liveliness. The commonest diagnosis in a paediatric clinic is the state "common anxious restlessness", which corresponds with the condition "hypomania" in adults, and which points to denial of the central depression. It could be said that the achievement of capacity for depression is under threat, and the child manages to retain the capacity by organisation of the denial of it. The alternative would be a serious setback in emotional development to a state that existed before integration, and therefore before the achievement of the "depressive position"; in other words madness.

As we watch older children we meet with organised manic-depressive illness, which doubly resembles that which appears in adults; but here we are meeting with something unusual, namely organised illness. Common anxious restlessness (hypomania) is (by contrast) a clinical state that can show in almost normal children, and it has no sharp line between it and the well-recognised lability of infancy and early childhood, a period of life in which tears are mingled with great joy, and joy is tempered with grief.

The central fact denied in manic defence is death in the inner world, or a deadness over all; and the accent, in the manic defence, is on life, liveliness, denial of death as an ultimate fact of life.

An understanding of the relation of mood swing to the central core of capacity for concern in the personality is of very great value in the understanding of ordinary childhood behaviour both in the home and at school.

CHAPTER 3

Various types of
psycho-therapy material

I N D O I N G P S Y C H O - A N A L Y S I S one is constantly on the look out for indications as to the main source of the material presented for interpretation.*

At this point it may help the reader to consider the types of material presented by patients in analysis. These types can be sorted out, although in conducting a treatment the analyst is always ready for a mixture of types. First it is necessary to indicate the way in which a treatment starts, so that it becomes differentiated sharply from play therapy, and from group activities of all kinds. In psycho-analysis (apart from analysis adapted to the needs of the psychotic patient) a treatment starts when the first interpretation is made which brings to consciousness some element in the material presented which was capable of presentation yet not fully accepted by the patient.

For instance, a boy of 3 takes three bricks and makes a tunnel, then takes two trains and makes them collide in the tunnel; interpretation: inside you people meet and you hold them and make them bash, or keep them apart; you are telling me about mother and father, and the way they love each other or quarrel and you seem left out of it all. (The boy developed acute asthma as he bashed the trains together and the interpretation, given in this case within three minutes of the start of the analysis, immediately relieved the asthma attack.) It will be observed that this was not a transference interpretation; as analyst I simply cashed in, at this early date, on the belief in people that the boy brought with him. The boy brought to the treatment certain expecta-

---

* *Note for revision:* psycho-analysis starts with patient + → develop theme to unconscious co-operation process, growth and use of intimacy, self-revelation, "surprises".

tions based on the parents' attitudes to which he was already accustomed, and also perhaps influenced by what he had been told about coming to treatment. Nevertheless once I had made this interpretation the treatment had started and all the subsequent material was influenced by the fact that I had entered the boy's life as a human being who can put things into words, who can deal objectively with the situation that is full of feeling, who can tolerate conflict and who can see what is just ready in the patient to become conscious and therefore acceptable as a self phenomenon.

In this particular case if the interpretation had not been made the child would have gone home with asthma and the treatment would have failed at the beginning. In many cases, however, there is no hurry; the child has an idea of coming to treatment which can be used by the analyst while he gathers the information gradually before deciding what kind of interpretation will best set the deeper work of the treatment in motion.

The co-operation of the patient is in the main an unconscious one, but the type of material presented depends on the language of the analyst. The patient (however young) appreciates the way the analyst most easily works, and can most easily be hoodwinked.

The stuff of the analysis (child or adult) can roughly be classified into types:*

(1) External relationships as between whole people.

(2) Samples of the inner world and the variations on the theme of a fantasy life placed either within or without.

(3) Intellectualised material in terms of which work can be done, but this work needs to be repeated in another form with feeling in it in the transference relationship.

(4) Material principally indicating the structural weaknesses of the Ego, and the threat of loss of capacity for relationship, and the threat of unreality and depersonalisation.

---

* *Note for revision:* Add classification via environment.

(1) The analysis of this material is along the lines of the language of my first section, with interpretation of the nascent conscious in the transference situation; the stuff of the analysis is the instinctual experience and fantasy that is elaborated round physical function, and the aim of the analyst is a quantitative lessening of the work of repression. The special conditions of the analytic setting enable the patient to organise and to socialise the new potential that results when the work of repression is lessened.

As an example of this material I take a detail from the analysis of the same small boy. On one occasion he came up the stairs to the treatment room, giving me the warning "I am God". I knew therefore that I was to expect to be used as a bad person who ought to be punished. The intensity of the feeling was tremendous. He had soon manoeuvred the situation so that he was standing on a table in the centre of the room and I was far enough away for him to be able to deceive me. In spite of the special care that I was taking I found myself hit between the eyes with a stick that he had secreted. He had identified himself with a powerful and strict person of his inner world and had used me to represent himself as the son in the Oedipus triangle and I had to be killed. Here again interpretation had to be made quickly before secondary considerations arose such as the idea that he ought to feel sorry for hurting me. In the actual material there was no room for grief or guilt. Similar material of a less anxious kind had shown me the exact meaning of what happened at this tense moment and on other occasions the roles had been reversed so that his anxiety had been great. It could be said of this material, as of any, that to some extent it was a sample of inner world life. Nevertheless in the main it was an expression of the unconscious fantasy in the interpersonal relationship with both himself and myself as whole persons.

(2) As an example of inner world material presented in analysis I will take the play of a child in which the table is specifically used and the play is for the time being confined to the limits set by the table. It is taken for granted that there is a world unrepresented in the sample. Nevertheless there is a life expressed in the sample as if a chapter of a novel were being written. There are good and bad figures and there are

representatives of all the mechanisms of defence characteristic of the inner world of a child who has achieved integration and has taken over responsibility for a collection of memories and feelings and instincts which constitute the self. Perhaps violent things happen and the boundaries are overstepped but the disruption of the boundaries is important as a phenomenon in itself. Often a child will have the room somewhat darkened and it is fairly obvious that the analyst is within the inside of the child and is there playing one role and then another according to directions from the child. The world is ruled by magic and magical control is represented by the child's verbal directions which control the analyst and which transfigure the objects in the room and which alter the rules according to the child's whim. When the room is transformed in this way so that the walls represent the boundaries of the child's Ego, to some extent the external world is also altered by being shut out. There is no easy transition from within to without and the end of the hour becomes a matter for skilful management. In the case of the withdrawn child the analyst comes into a world which is artificially benign, malign forces and objects having been placed outside. In such a case the analyst is caught up in an endless series of magical actions and it is strange to the child that the analyst does not know what is expected. The child can fly and of course the analyst is expected to take the child around the room and up to the nest at the top of the cupboard. Outside the room in this case are all the forces of persecution lying in wait, and the slightest sound may cause terror. Accidental intrusion into the room by a third person can be disastrous and the end of the hour requires very special treatment. This inner world material is affected by the presence of the analyst within it, especially as the analyst becomes able to understand very quickly what is required and therefore is able to play into the child's need for magical control. The analyst who retains an objectivity and a sense of reality which the child has lost, while playing various roles in a very sensitive way according to need, acknowledges both the child's need for magic and the need for the facts that belong to external reality. Caught up in this inner world material, the analyst has a limited scope for interpretation of the phenomena met with. Nevertheless in the course of the hour there are occasions in which details of this inner

world can be related to the phenomena of the child's external relationships, either the instinctual life of the child as a whole human
being or else the life the child has met with in the last 24 hours and has
introjected.

It is when playing with a child who is presenting this sort of
material that the analyst sees the inadequacy of the term fantasy, an
inadequacy which analysts have tried to get round by spelling the word
phantasy to indicate the unconscious quality. This is not, however,
satisfactory, especially as the fantasy is not altogether unconscious.
The term psychic reality expresses the analyst's understanding that
the fantasy presented by the patient is real in its own sense and is far
removed from that which is called fantasying, which is to some extent
under conscious control and from which the unwanted elements are
sieved out. In the material of psychic reality there is no place for denial
since material that is eliminated must yet be placed somewhere.

(3) An example of intellectualised material would be the phases in an
analysis in which a child, just like a grownup, reports dreams, asks
questions, and expects an objective discussion of a situation. In some
analyses the work is done chiefly in these terms, especially with adults
and adolescents. Even small children make use of the analyst in this
way from time to time, but this work is preparatory work and makes
use of the more direct expression which appears gradually and obviously in the small child's play. The difference between the analysis of a
small child and that of an adult is that with the small child most of the
acting out is in the form of play in the treatment hour, whereas with an
adult almost all the acting out may be in the adult's life external to the
analysis, the work of the analysis being done verbally. The analyst is
prepared, however, for the small child in the adult as well as for the
adult in the small child.

(4) As an example of play material indicating anxiety in regard to Ego
structure, I give the case of a boy of 6 whose maniacal outbursts
indicated a violent disintegration. He used a round table and he put
houses all round the edge and then he put another row of houses
within. Inside the second row there was room for little life. One could
have interpreted the details of this life but the main interpretation was

concerned with the over-emphasis of the body or Ego boundary. Corresponding with this the boy was developing a very much exaggerated personality. On another occasion he used many compartments on the mantelpiece, placing a sample of inner world life in each compartment, there being no relationship allowed between them (dissociation as a defence).

A girl of 6, who had recovered from a psychotic phase in which I was able to help her a year previously, returned to my room at her own request, bringing her sister. Whereas the sister took the toys and played like an ordinary child, this girl who had been my patient made a long row of houses creating a road that stretched the whole width of my room. I was able to find out that she was joining up my house with hers which was about 10 miles away and at the same time joining the past with the present and indicating the strain that she had had in maintaining a relationship with me over the year since the end of the treatment.

Material relating to the indwelling of the psyche in the body takes many forms. Sometimes the body gets hurt or becomes excited or is clearly indicated in the play setting. An affectionate contact between the patient and the analyst may become a feature and needs to be interpreted because it is produced for a purpose like any other material of an analysis. Pretence eating of food or food actually brought and consumed may have the same sort of significance, or there may be sexual advances of a more direct kind. The child who has learned to expect interpretation of the material presented becomes amazingly free to produce material of any kind whatever according to the need of the hour.

CHAPTER 4

HYPOCHONDRIACAL
ANXIETY

THE THEORETICIAN'S conception of the human being in terms of a limiting membrane, with an inside and an outside, is at the same time a drawing that the infant might make of the self, or a fellow-human. The infant is concerned about an inside, and about the inside phenomena to which I have referred, and is concerned about the body and about the psyche at the same time. It is just here that the term psycho-somatic begins to have a special meaning.

At first there is the simple identity of the body and the psyche, from the points of view of the baby. Here starts a state of affairs in which *ill-health* is identical with *doubt* about oneself. For the hypochondriac of any age the trouble is doubt and not disease. It is a matter of the balance of the forces of "good" and "evil" within, and this is true for the infant and for the psycho-somatic sufferer, and for the more sophisticated philosophical doubter.

The health of the body, in so far as it is felt or noticed, is translated into fantasy, and at the same time the phenomena of fantasy are felt in terms of body. For instance, guilt-feeling may be expressed as vomiting, or vomiting (perhaps with physical cause) may be felt to have betrayed the secret inner self and so to have been a disaster. Apart from disease, bodily health is actively reassuring to the infant who is coping with doubts about the psyche; and psyche health promotes healthy body functioning, with capacity for ingestion, digestion, elimination.

It is to this point in development that the psycho-somatic research worker should come for an examination of the roots of his subject. Here is to be found the basis for the study of the vast subject of the inter-relationship of physical and psychological disorders. The psy-

chiatrist can here find an explanation for many phenomena of depression and hypochondria (also paranoia – see later) and also he finds in
psychiatry of infancy a kind of psychiatry that is yet relatively little
muddled up by the subsidiary phenomena of "mental" disease or
"intellectual" secondary formations. The psycho-analyst naturally
looks here with the very greatest interest; in the study of conversion
hysteria there is something to be gained from an examination of the
infant's original mix-up of the body itself with the feeling and ideas
about the body.

PART IV

FROM INSTINCT THEORY
TO EGO THEORY

INTRODUCTION:
PRIMITIVE
EMOTIONAL DEVELOPMENT

SOMEWHAT ARTIFICIALLY I shall choose three different languages for the description of the earlier phenomena of emotional development.* First I shall discuss

A. The establishment of a relationship with external reality,

then B. The integration of the unit self from an unintegrated state†

and C. The lodgement of the psyche in the body.

I can find no clear sequence in development that can be used to determine the order of description.

It will be noted that as we get further and further back in our study of the developing human being so we become more and more obviously and deeply involved in a study of environment, which in terms of psycho-therapy is management. Yet for the sake of clarity I have decided to deal with this large subject, the external factor, in one chapter (pp.152 ff), since whatever the degree of importance we may assign to environment, the individual remains, and makes sense of environment.

---

* See Winnicott, D.W.: (1945) "Primitive Emotional Development", an alternative presentation of this theme.
† *Note for revision:* Unintegration ↔ integration

ESTABLISHMENT OF RELATIONSHIP WITH EXTERNAL REALITY

EXCITED AND QUIET RELATIONSHIPS

I T I S C O N V E N I E N T to separate off two aspects of this subject from each other, "excited" relationships and "quiet" relationships.

All the time we have a baby in mind. Let us imagine a theoretical first feed. Here is a baby with developing instinct tension. There develops an expectancy, a state of affairs in which the infant is prepared to find something somewhere, not knowing what. There is no comparable expectancy in the quiet or unexcited state. At about the right moment the mother offers her breast.*

If the mother is able to be preoccupied with her task she is able to provide the setting for the start of excited relationships, because she is biologically orientated exactly to this job.

This theoretical first feed is also an actual first feed, except that in real experience it is not so much a matter of a single happening as a build-up of memories of events. It may be said that because of the extreme immaturity of the newborn babe the first feed cannot be significant as an emotional experience. Yet there is no doubt that if the first feed goes well, contact is established, so that the pattern of the subsequent feeds develops out of this first experience, then the task of the mother is immensely simplified. *Per contra*, if the first feeds are mishandled, then a great deal of trouble may be caused and, in fact, a lasting pattern of insecurity of relationship may be found to have started at the time of the early failure of management.

---

* The subject is complex enough, and I shall not make it worse by allowing for breast-substitutes and mother-substitutes.

At the (theoretical) first feed the baby is ready to create, and the mother makes it possible for the baby to have the illusion that the breast, and what the breast means, has been created by impulse out of need.

DIAGRAM 3

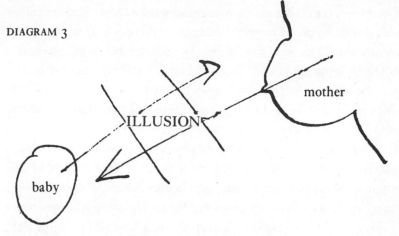

Of course we as sophisticated philosophers know that what the baby created was not that which the mother presented, but the mother by her extremely delicate adaptation to the (emotional) needs of the infant is able to allow the baby this illusion. Without her being "good" enough in this respect the infant can have no hope whatever of a capacity for excited relationship with objects or people in what we as observers call the real world, external or shared reality, the world not created by the infant.

At first, then, there is almost exact adaptation to need, affording the infant the illusion of having created external objects. The mother gradually decreases in her capacity for adaptation to (emotional) need, but the infant has ways and means of dealing with this change. It is misleading to think of the establishment of the infant's reality sense in terms of the mother's insistence on the externality of external things. In the language of this chapter the key-words are illusion and disillusionment. Illusion must first be given, after which the infant has plenty of means for acceping and even making use of disillusionment.

These excited experiences take place against a background of quietude, in which there is another kind of relationship between the baby and the mother. We are concerned with an infant in a highly dependent state and totally unaware of this dependence. It is a legitimate simplification to assume the presence of the mother, which provides the environment which is an essential part of dependence. Where there is total dependence there is accurate adaptation; or in other words, with failure of maternal adaptation there is a distortion of the infant's individual processes of life. The mother has been responsible for the environment in a physical way before the birth of the infant, and after the birth the mother continues with the provision of physical care which is the only kind of expression of love that the infant can at first appreciate. Innumerable rehearsals of adaptation and failure of adaptation have taken place already by the time we can postulate a theoretical first feed. At the time of this theoretical first feed the baby has already certain expectations and certain experiences which to a greater or a lesser degree complicate the situation. Where the complications are not too great something very simple happens. It is difficult to find the right words to describe this simple event; but it can be said that by reason of an aliveness in the infant and through the development of instinct tension the infant comes to expect something; and then there is a reaching out which can soon take the form of an impulsive movement of the hand or a movement of the mouth towards a presumed object. I think it is not out of place to say that the infant is ready to be creative. There would be a hallucination of an object if there were memory material for use in the process of creation but this cannot be postulated in consideration of the theoretical first feed. Here the new human being is in the position of creating the world. The motive is personal need; we witness need gradually changing over into desire.

The mother who has been able to meet the more primitive needs by the simple fact of physical care is now in a new role. She has to meet a specific creative moment and to know about this through her own capacity for identification with the infant and by her observation of the infant's behaviour. The mother is waiting to be discovered and she need not have an intellectual appreciation of the fact that she has to be created by the infant, to play her part and to be created by each infant anew.

The mother who has just been through a gruelling experience

herself has an extremely difficult task. She herself has to be ready with a kind of potency so that neither the overfull breast nor the completely quiescent breast is exactly appropriate. She is greatly helped by the experience of the genital potency of her man. Somehow or other she manages to be ready with a potential excitement which results eventually in the giving of milk. She will not be expected to be exactly accurate in her adaptation here. Fortunately the infant does not need an exact pattern of behaviour. When all goes well the infant is able to discover the nipple and this in itself is a tremendous event apart altogether from feeding. It is very important theoretically that the infant *creates* this object, and what the mother does is to place the nipple of her breast just there and at the right time so that it is her nipple that the baby creates. It is no doubt very important for the mother that the baby discovers the nipple in this way, creatively. Such a delicate initiation of a relationship requires certain conditions and it must be admitted that the right conditions are not usually present because of the general tendency in the maternity ward to ignore this which is so fundamental and so vital in the beginning of the relationship of the infant to what we already know is the world in which the infant will live.

Although the infant's capacity for excited relationships is built up through the summation of feeds (and other types of excited experience) yet in a theoretical discussion the first feed is the prototype, and in practice it is towards the better management of the first feed that we should direct our efforts.

When all goes well the relationship may be established in a few moments, and on the other hand when there is a difficulty the mother and the infant may take a long time to come to terms with each other and it is not at all uncommon for a mother and infant to fail from the beginning, and to suffer (each of them) from the results of this failure for many years, if not always.

We must expect a percentage of failures, since babies are of all kinds, and mothers are not all ready, at the right moment, for the exercise of their breast potency. Nevertheless it is not at all unusual for a failure at this point, disastrous for the development of the infant, to be unnecessary; the baby was ready and the mother was ready but the conditions were not satisfactory, or someone interfered. Here we come to the psychology of the doctors and nurses who are engaged in the care of mothers who have just given birth, and of the newborn babies themselves. There is no special preparation of nurses who are specially concerned with this early stage of the infant's life and with the care of the mothers in the first weeks after parturition. It is noticeable that this matter of the initial relationship between the infant and the mother rouses great anxiety in many ordinary healthy women, and it would be difficult otherwise to explain the frequency with which nurses who are otherwise skilled and kind tend to assume responsibility that should be the mother's, tend to take the matter into their own hands, and in fact try to force babies to the breast. It is not rare to find nurses, with the best will in the world, taking a baby well wrapped up in the blanket so that the hands are not available, shoving the baby's mouth on to the breast, and openly avowing that they are determined that they will *make the baby take.*

Here if anywhere theory and practice come right into line with each other. Most of these nurses are anxious not because they are neurotic but because no one has told them about the baby creating the breast, and about the mother's specific orientation to the task of adaptation to need, to the art of giving the infant the illusion that what is created out of need and by impulse has real existence.

It must be added that a proportion of nurses understand this intuitively, and take a pleasure in creating conditions in which the baby and the mother can come to terms with each other.

It is quite a practical matter. The way to get an infant to be inhibited in regard to breast feeding, and indeed in regard to feeding at all, is to introduce the breast to the baby without giving any opportunity for the baby to be the creator of the object which is to be found. There is perhaps no one detail which the psychologist can teach which if accepted would have a more profound effect on the mental health of the individuals of the community than this matter of the need for the infant to be the creator of the nipple of the breast of the mother. It is not merely a question, moreover, of the subsequent mental health of the new individual.

It may be that the words used are wrong. Perhaps the word "creation" can be supplanted by another which will be more universally understood or acceptable. The words do not matter. Ways must be found of drawing the attention of those who have charge of newly born babies to the tremendous importance of the initial experience of an excited relationship between the infant and the mother. There are inherent difficulties. Nurses and doctors are vitally important to the mother on account of what they can do for her to make labour safe and to give her physical help when she is worn out. They have their own skills, learned gradually and with difficulty. There is no reason why these same nurses and doctors should be able to give to the mother the role which is hers and which she alone can perform. All that the nurse can do in this situation is to set up the conditions in which the mother can be at her most sensitive. What the mother needs is a chance to be natural and to find her way with the baby in the way that mothers have found their way since the dawn of human history, and indeed before the evolution of man from mammal.

It will be seen that from the nurse's point of view the initial contact between the baby and the mother can look like play; indeed it could be called play, and the nurse in charge can easily feel that what is needed is work. Nevertheless the baby does not immediately need milk and this is well known in paediatrics. The baby who has discovered the nipple and whose mother is available to supply the nipple there near the hand or the mouth at the right moments is able to take time if necessary in starting to suck. There may be a period of chewing and from the start individual babies have their own techniques which may persist and show later on as mannerisms. The study of this initiation of a relationship must reward the observer richly. The important part of Merrill Middlemore's work, which was published in the book called *The Nursing Couple* [1941], is her description of the immense care she took to be present in the feeding situation without being in any way a disturber either of the nurses or of the mothers or of the babies. She took care not be expecting successes or afraid of failure. There must be very few who are equipped to make this type of observation of intimacy.

The theoretical first feed is represented in real life by the summation of the early experiences of many feeds. After the theoretical first feed the baby begins to have material with which to create. Gradually it can be said that the baby is ready to hallucinate the nipple at the time when the mother is ready with it. Memories are built up from innumerable sense-impressions associated with the activity of feeding and of finding the object. In the course of time there comes a state in which the infant feels confident that the object of desire can be found, and this means that the infant gradually tolerates the absence of the object. Thus starts the infant's concept of external reality, a place from which objects appear and in which they disappear. Through the magic of desire one can say that the baby has the illusion of magical creative power, and omnipotence is a fact through the sensitive adaptation of the mother. The basis for the infant's gradual recognition of a lack of magical control over external reality lies in the initial omnipotence that is made a fact by the mother's adaptive technique.

In the day to day life of infancy we can watch the infant exploiting this third or illusory world which is neither inner reality nor external fact, and which we allow to the infant although we do not allow it to the adult or even to an older child. We see the infant sucking fingers or adopting a technique of twiddling the face or murmuring a sound or clutching a piece of cloth, and we know that the infant is claiming magical control over the world in these ways, prolonging (and we allow it) the omnipotence that was met and so implemented originally by the mother's adapting. I have thought it useful to call the objects and phenomena that belong to this kind of experience "transitional". I have called the objects used "transitional objects" and the techniques employed "transitional phenomena". These terms imply that there is a temporary state belonging to early infancy in which the infant is allowed to claim magical control over external reality, a control which we know is made real by the mother's adapting, but the infant does not yet know this. The "transitional object" or first possession is an object which the infant has created, although at the same time that we say this we actually know it to have been a bit of blanket or a fringe of a shawl or a Harrington square. The next possession will have been given to the baby by an aunt and for this the child must say "ta", thereby acknow-ledging a limitation of magical control and acknowledging dependence on the goodwill of people in the external world.

How important then are these early transitional objects and techniques! Their importance is reflected in their persistence, even crude persistence over the years. Out of these transitional phenomena develop much of what we variously allow and greatly value under the headings of religion and art and also the little madnesses which are legitimate at the moment, according to the prevailing cultural pattern.

There is a no-man's-land between the subjective and what is objectively perceived that is natural to infancy, and this we expect and allow. The infant is not challenged at first, does not have to decide, can be allowed to claim of something that is borderline that it is at one and the same time self-created and perceived or accepted from the world, the world that existed before the conception of the infant. Someone claiming indulgence in this respect at a later age is called mad. In religion and in the arts, we see the claim socialised so that the individual is not called mad and can enjoy in the exercise of religion or the practice and appreciation of the arts the rest that human beings need from absolute and never-failing discrimination between fact and fantasy.*

FAILURE IN
INITIAL CONTACT

I will now study the effect of failure rather than of success, the state that arises either when the mother is unable to meet the infant's desires in a sufficiently sensitive manner or when the infant is too disturbed (because of earlier experiences) to surrender to the instinctual urge.

In the matter of practical management the infant who fails to make contact with external reality does not usually die. By the persistence of those in care the infant becomes seduced into feeding and living, although the basis for living is feeble or absent. In terms of psychologi-cal theory the failure at this point exaggerates instead of healing a split in the person of the infant. Instead of the relationship with external

---

* [This paragraph was found separately typed with a note that it should be added.]

reality softened by the temporary use of an illusory state of omnipotence there develop two separate kinds of object relationship, and
these two can be so unrelated as to constitute a serious illness which
must eventually show in clinical schizophrenia. On the one hand there
is the infant's private life in which relationships are based on the
infant's capacity to create rather than on the memory of contacts, and
on the other hand there is a false self which develops on a compliance
basis and is related in a passive way to the demands of external reality.
It is very easy to be deceived and to see a baby responding to skilful
feeding, and to fail to notice that this infant who takes in an entirely
passive way has never created the world, and has no capacity for
external relationships, and has no future as an individual. The exploitation of this compliant false self cannot lead to a good result. The true
self can only show as a refusal to feed. The infant stays alive and it is
surprising how satisfied doctors can be with the result. The false self
becomes organised to keep the world at bay, and there is another and
true self hidden away and therefore protected. This true self is in a
constant state of what might be called internal relatedness. Clinically,
evidence of the internal life of the hidden self may show in rocking
movements and other signs of very primitive life.

A description of the extreme degree of the splitting leads the way
to a description of the lesser degrees of splitting and indeed of the way
in which some degree of what is being described is present in all
children and is inherent in life itself. In the extreme degree the child
has no reason for living at all but in the commoner lesser degrees there
is some degree of a sense of futility in regard to the false living, and a
constant search for the life that feels real, even if it leads to death, as by
starvation. In the lesser degrees there are objects in the secret inner
relatedness of the true self and these objects have been derived from
some degree of success at the stage of the theoretical first feed. In other
words, in the lesser degrees of this illness it is not so much the primary
state of splitting which is to be found as a secondary organisation of
splitting which implies regression from difficulties encountered at a
later stage of emotional development.

By using the diagram that belongs to the extreme case one can easily illustrate the implications of this way of looking at early emotional development and apply what we see to the task of the ordinary normal person and the difficulties inherent in life.*

It is instructive to take the task of the artist and to describe this task in the terms set out in this chapter. In this way one can say that there are two types of artist. One kind of artist operates at first from the false self, that which can only too easily make an exact representation of a sample of external reality. The artist makes use of this ability and what we next see is the attempt of the true self in the artist to relate the first exact impression to the crude phenomena that constitute aliveness in the secret true self. If there is success the artist has not only produced something recognisable to others but also something which is individual to the artist's true self; the finished product has value because we can appreciate the struggle that has gone on in the artist in the work of drawing together the elements originally separated. If the skill in technique runs away with the artist we use the word facile and speak of a virtuoso.

In contrast to this is the other kind of artist who starts off with crude representations of the secret self phenomena or personal aliveness which are pregnant with meaning for the artist but at first have no meaning for others. The artist's task in this case is to make his very personal representations intelligible, and in order to do this he

---

* [An alternative version to some of the foregoing was found separately typed with a note that it should be added at this point. It reads:]

"When there is a certain degree of failure of adaptation, or a chaotic adaptation, the infant develops two types of relationship. One type is a silent secret relationship to an essentially personal and private inner world of subjective phenomena, and it is only this relationship that seems real. The other is from a false self to a dimly perceived external or implanted environment. The first contains the spontaneity and the richness, and the second is a relationship of compliance kept up for gaining time till perhaps the first may some day come into its own. It is surprisingly easy, clinically, to miss the unreality of the compliance half of a schizophrenic child's technique for living.

The trouble is that the impulses and the spontaneity and the feelings that seem real are all bound up in a relationship that is (in extreme degree) incommunicable. On the other hand, the other half of the split personality, the compliant false self, is plain for all the world to see, and easy to manage."

must betray himself to some extent. His artistic creations seem to him like so many failures, however much they are appreciated by the coterie; and in fact if they are appreciated too widely the artist may withdraw altogether because of the sense of having been false to his true self. Here again, the main achievement of the artist is his work of integration of the two selves. The first type of artist is appreciated by persons who have a need to get into touch with their crude impulses, whereas the second type is appreciated by those who are withdrawn, and who are relieved to find there can be some (though not too much) sharing of what is basically personal, and essentially secret.

PRIMARY CREATIVITY   Is there or is there not a primary creativity? Or, on the other hand, is the human being only capable of projection of that which has been previously introjected, or (in other language) of excreting what has been incorporated?

What is the answer to the problem of creativity? At the theoretical first feed, for instance, has the infant no contribution to make?

At least until we know more I must assume that there is a creative potential, and that at the theoretical first feed the baby has a personal contribution to make. If the mother adapts well enough the baby assumes that the nipple and the milk are the results of a gesture that arose out of need, the result of an idea that rode in on the crest of a wave of instinctual tension. In my opinion these matters are of great practical significance for the psychiatrist, and also for the paediatrician in his clinical work.

If there is a true creative potential then we must expect to find it, along with projection of introjected detail, in all productive effort, and we shall distinguish the creative potential not so much by the original-ity in the production as by the individual's sense of the reality of the experience and of the object.

The world is created anew by each human being, who starts on the task at least as early as at the time of birth and of the theoretical first feed. What the infant creates is very largely dependent on what is presented to that infant at the moment of creativity, by the mother who makes active adaptation to the infant's needs, but if the creativity of the infant is absent, the details presented by the mother are meaningless.

We know that the world was there before the infant, but the infant does not know this, and at first the infant has the illusion that what is found is created. But this state of affairs is only achieved when the mother acts well enough. This problem of primary creativity has been discussed as one of earliest infancy; in point of fact it is a problem that never ceases to have meaning, as long as the individual is alive.*

Gradually there comes about an intellectual understanding of the fact of the world's existence prior to the individual's, but feeling remains that the world is personally created.

I put great stress on this part of the study of human nature. Several matters that at first examination seem to be unrelated are found to meet at this very point. To enumerate:

A. The practical matter of the management of the mother and infant in the first hours and days after a baby is born (paediatrics).

B. The relationship of excited bodily relationships to quiet relationships in general, including the problems that belong to marriage.

C. The philosophical problem of the meaning of the word "real".

D. The religious claim linked to that of the arts, for illusion as something valuable in its own right.

E. The unreality feelings of schizoid people and of insane schizophrenics.

F. The claim of the psychotic that what is not real is real, and the claim of the antisocial child that what is untrue is true and that dependence (which is a fact) is not a fact.

G. The essential split in schizophrenia, prophylaxis against which is a matter of management at the earliest stage of infantile emotional development, when need must be met by sensitive adaptation to need.

---

* *Note for revision:* Here draw on play, cultural location etc.

H. The concept of primary creativity, and of absolute originality, as against the projection of previously introjected (digested and worked over) objects and phenomena.

THE MOTHER'S   To some extent it is true that the needs of
IMPORTANCE   an infant can be supplied by anyone who
                    loves the infant, but there are two sets of
reasons why the mother is the right person.

Her love of her own infant is likely to be more true, less sentimental, than that of any substitute; an extreme adaptation to the infant's needs can be made by the real mother without resentment. The actual mother will be able to continue with all her little details of personal technique, thus providing the infant with a simplified emotional (which includes physical) environment. A baby that is beautifully cared for by several different people, or even by two, has a much more complex beginning to life, a much less sure background of things to be taken for granted when desires appear as complications from within.

A good deal of confusion can arise out of neglect of this consideration. It is true, as Anna Freud points out, that techniques are the important things that affect the baby at the beginning. But simplicity and continuity of technique can only be given by one person who is acting naturally; and no one but the mother is likely to be able to supply this, unless it be a suitable adoptive mother taking over care from the very beginning. But the adoptive mother usually lacks the real mother's orientation to motherhood, or special state that needs the full preparatory period of nine months.

It is not easy for mothers to express their feelings about their experiences in maternity wards and nursing homes, in spite of the fact that they have very strong feelings indeed, not always happy. To some extent mothers lose the intensity of their feelings when the experience becomes a few months away in the past; also they know as they get further away from the actual experience of labour that at that special time there is a liability to imagine, almost to hallucinate, a persecutory woman figure, so that a bad experience is seen in retrospect as if it were a bad dream. But the bad experiences are often only too real, since there is so poor an understanding of the mother's special task of introducing the world to her baby.

Nevertheless, women who have an understanding friend with whom to talk throughout the period covering several labours do find they have a great deal to say about the obstacles that exist preventing a mother from coming to terms with her infant in her own way.

It is certainly a very great help when the infant is in a crib beside the mother's bed as in the scheme described by Spence. It must be difficult for a nurse to remember that a mother who is perhaps too weak to lift her baby out of the bedside crib unaided is nevertheless the right person and the only right person for adapting to the infant's needs, needs which are indicated in ways that call specifically on the actual mother's subtlety of understanding.

THE BABY AT BIRTH   There seems to be a difference between the emotional needs of infants born at full term and those of infants born prematurely. Also it must be expected that the post-mature infant will be liable to be born in a state of frustration. Undoubtedly, the right time for birth from the standpoint of emotional needs is the time of full term, a fact which might have been predicted.

To the paediatrician an apology is due, that these matters bypass all the careful work done on the physiology and biochemistry and haematology of the newborn, and of the feeding function. The fact is that in most cases physical health can now be taken for granted (because of the paediatricians' work), and the result is health, and health in child care is not the end but the beginning. Infants could not be studied in their development until the fear of physical disease and disorder had been cleared away. Now we can see that healthy development is not a matter of weight-watching but a matter of emotional development. The study of emotional development, as I hope I am showing, is a vast and complex matter.

It is not useful to refer to a first feed as an instinctual experience taking place and ending with no reference to the human being in whom the excitement is taking place. At first the infant is not able to accept the experience and assimilate to the self the full result of instinctual events. There was an unexcited state that was disturbed by the excited one. This quiet state surely is the primary one, and deserves study in its own right.

A very great deal in the quality of this quiet state is taken for granted in the assumption that an infant has been (physically) well cared for, in the womb before birth, and in general management after birth. We can profitably study the results of failure of physical care, and so try to deduce what is actually done by successful care, apart from satisfaction of instinctual demands.

THE PHILOSOPHY OF "REAL"

Philosophers have always been concerned with the meaning of the word "real", and there have been schools of thought founded on the belief that

> "this stone and this tree
> discontinue to be
> when there's no one about in the quad"

with the alternative:

> "this stone and this tree
> do continue to be
> as observed by yours faithfully . . ."

It is not every philosopher who sees that this problem that besets every human being is a description of the initial relationship to external reality at the theoretical first feed; or for that matter at any theoretical first contact.

I would put it this way. Some babies are fortunate enough to have a mother whose initial active adaptation to their infant's need was good enough. This enables them to have the illusion of actually finding what was created (hallucinated). Eventually, after a capacity for relationships has been established, such babies can take the next step towards recognition of the essential aloneness of the human being. Eventually such a baby grows up to say "I know that there is no direct contact between external reality and myself, only an illusion of contact, a midway phenomenon that works very well for me when I am not tired. I couldn't care less that there is a philosophical problem involved."

Babies with slightly less fortunate experiences are really bothered by the idea of there being no direct contact with external reality. A sense of threat of loss of capacity for relationships hangs over them all the time. For them the philosophical problem becomes and remains a vital one, a matter of life and death, of feeding or starvation, of love or isolation.

Even more unfortunate babies whose early experiences of having the world properly introduced were confused grow up with no capacity for illusion of contact with external reality; or their capacity is so slight that it breaks down at a time of frustration and schizoid illness develops.

CHAPTER 2

INTEGRATION

I N THE FORMULATION of psychological theory it is only too easy to take integration for granted, but in a study of the early stages of the developing human individual it is necessary to think of integration as an achievement. No doubt there is a biological tendency towards integration, but in psychological studies of human nature it is never satisfactory to lean too heavily on the biological aspect of growth.

Clinically in psychiatry we are familiar with the process of disintegration, an active undoing of integration, brought about and perhaps organised in defence against anxiety associated with integration. The direct study of disintegration can be misleading, however, to the student of the processes of integration.

It is necessary to postulate an unintegrated state out of which integration takes place. The infant that we know as a human unit, safe in the womb, is not yet a unit in terms of emotional development. If we examine [this] from the infant's point of view (although the infant is not there, as such, to have a point of view), unintegration is accompanied by unawareness.

At the theoretical start is an unintegrated state,* a lack of wholeness both in space and time. At this stage there is no awareness. As soon as we talk of *a collection* of impulses and sensations we have gone further forward than the beginning, when the centre of gravity (so to speak) of the self shifts from one impulse or sensation to another. The beginning is certainly at some date prior to full-term birth.

---

* These ideas derive from Edward Glover and his concept of "ego-nuclei", but the reader should consult Glover's own work rather than rely on my personal account, as I am not setting out to describe his contribution.

Out of the unintegrated state comes integration for moments or brief periods, and only gradually does a general state of integration become a fact. Promoting integration are internal factors such as instinctual urge or aggressive expression, each of which is preceded by a gathering together of the whole self. Awareness becomes possible at such moments, because there is a self to be aware. Integration is also promoted by the environmental care. In psychology it must be said that the infant falls to pieces unless held together, and physical care is psychological care at these stages.

The mother knows by empathy that when a baby is picked up time must be taken over the process. The baby must receive warning; the parts of the body are gathered together; eventually, at the right point in time, the child is airborne; moreover the mother's act starts, continues and ends, for the baby is being lifted from one place to another, perhaps from the cot to the mother's shoulder.

As the self becomes established and the individual becomes able to incorporate and hold memories of environmental care, and therefore to be capable of self-care, so integration becomes a more reliable state. Thus dependence becomes lessened. Gradually as integration becomes a maintained state of the individual so the word disintegration rather than unintegration becomes appropriate for description of the negative of integration. At later stages exaggerations of self-care can be seen, organised as a defence against the disintegration which environmental failure threatens to bring about. By environmental failure I mean failure of secure holding, and failure beyond that which can be borne at the time by the individual.

It is possible to detect disintegration which is occurring as an organised defence against the tremendous pain of various anxieties associated with the fully integrated state. Disintegration of this kind can be used later as a basis for a pathological chaotic state which is a secondary phenomenon, and which is not directly related to the primary chaos of the human individual.

In illustration of the application of these principles it is useful to think of the nursery rhyme of Humpty Dumpty and the reasons for its universal appeal. Evidently there is a general feeling, not available to consciousness, that integration is a precarious state. The nursery rhyme perhaps appeals because it acknowledges personal integration as an achievement.

In my description of the first integrations out of the unintegrated state the words that were used were arithmetical. It is a question whether the individual's ego-nuclei do or do not add up to one. It can sometimes be shown in a treatment that an inhibition in the use of ordinary simple arithmetic has derived from the individual child's inability to start off with a simple concept of one, the unit, which to be sensible must represent ultimately the self. It is notorious that an inability to do simple arithmetic by no means implies an inability to do extremely complex mental calculations of an abstract kind, and in fact there may be a relationship between an exaggerated use of abstract thinking in mathematical terms and an inhibition of simple addition and subtraction.

These theoretical considerations to some extent explain the value which is derived from both love and hate and even from reactive anger when these are expressed without reserve and at the moment of most acute feeling. Integration feels sane, and it feels mad to be losing integration that has been acquired. These urgent moments of surrender to self-expression have value in this matter of the integration which belongs to them. Closely associated with this problem of newly acquired integration, with unintegration behind, and disintegration as a threat in the future, is the exploitation of skin sensation, a dramatization of physical care, and an over-emphasis of the self-caring capacity which, in turn, is derived from a mixture of memories of being held and the experience of not being held quite enough.

In the life of the normal infant rest must be able to include relaxation and a regression to unintegration. Gradually as the self develops in strength and complexity this regression to unintegration becomes nearer and nearer to a painful state of "mad" disintegration. There is thus an intermediate stage in which a well-cared-for developing baby can relax and unintegrate, and tolerate (but only just tolerate) feeling "mad" in the unintegrated state. Then a stage forward is made, a step towards independence, and a loss for ever of the capacity to be unintegrated except in madness or in the specialised

conditions provided in psycho-therapy. After this the word is disintegration rather than unintegration.

The question as to whether a baby is better nursed or placed in a
cot can be examined at this point. Of course a baby needs both
experiences. Nevertheless it can be said that where the holding of a
baby is perfect (and it often is, since mothers know just how to do it)
then the baby can get confidence even in the live relationship, and can
unintegrate while being held. This is the richest type of experience.
Often, however, the holding is variable or even spoiled by anxiety
(mother's over-control against dropping) or by anxiousness (mother's
trembling, hot skin, over-acting heart, etc.) in which case the baby
cannot afford to relax. Relaxation then only comes with exhaustion. In
such a case the cradle or cot offers a welcome alternative. Provision has
to be made, however, for baby's return from relaxation (re-integra-
tion).

It is some factor like this one that makes some infants able to thrive
on the bottle, whereas breast feeding was impossible. So much
depends on the way the mother holds the baby, and let it be empha-
sised that this is not something that can be taught; if one can help it is
by giving the mother confidence in our management of environment
for her, and by our giving her opportunity for the exercise of her own
natural powers.

The clothes of an infant at the theoretical start can be a nuisance.
Immediately after birth the sensitivity of the skin is very high. There is
probably a place for rather primitive nakedness and for the uninter-
rupted body contact between baby and mother at the early stages, and
this has not been worked out as far as I know. Research along these
lines could follow naturally on the paediatric work with premature
infants, which points to the value of nakedness in incubator technique.* The fact is that integration and the attainment of unit status
brings great new developments in its train. Integration means
responsibility, and accompanied as it is by awareness, and by the
collection of memories, and by the bringing of the past, present and
future into a relationship, it almost means the beginning of human

---

* Mary Crosse: Birmingham. [A pioneer in neonatology.]

psychology. My statement of the depressive position in emotional development takes up the theme at this point. Unfortunately, much can happen that is untoward in the emotional development of an infant prior to this attainment of unit status, and for many infants the real human tasks of the so-called "depressive position" are never reached.

If (in one case) the accent is on *integration through good infant care*, the personality may be well founded. If the accent is on integration through *impulse and instinctual experience* and through the anger that maintains its relation to desire, then the personality is likely to be interesting, even exciting in quality. In health there is enough of each of these two, and the combination of the two spells stability. When there is not enough of either, integration is never well established, or is established in a set way, over-emphasised and heavily defended, and allowing of no relaxation, restful unintegration.

There is a third way of development, by which integration appears early and the accent is on excessive *reaction to impingement* from external sources. This is a result of failure of care, and will be discussed in a later section. Integration is here bought at a price, since impingement is expected and indeed continues to be needed, and a very early basis for a paranoid disposition (not inherited) is to be found in this not uncommon state of affairs.

As the child develops, so the word disintegration rather than unintegration must be used to describe loss of integration. Disintegration is an active defensive process, and is as much a defence against unintegration as against integration. Disintegration is along lines of cleavage set up by the organisation of the inner world and the control of inner objects and forces. In clinical work we meet disintegration of various degrees and types, well organised even in severe psychotic breakdown. Unintegration we only meet in the relaxation of healthy people, and in the deep regression which can be achieved in a psycho-therapy in which the organisation of defences is taken over from the patient by the therapist and is represented by the highly specialised physical and emotional conditions of the analytic situation.

It is here in this highly specialised psycho-therapy situation rather than by direct observation of infants that the state of affairs that is normal at the theoretical start in infancy can be studied.

There is an interesting observation to be made about the results of the actual fact of integration. Integration brings with it an expectation of attack. It appears that this is more true when the individual achieves integrations at a late date and less true for the original integrations of the normal infant. The gathering together of the elements of the self with the establishment of an external world produces for the time being a state of affairs that could be labelled paranoid. At such moments the mother's care is important in coming in between the integrated individual and the repudiated external world. Integration achievements at a late date, that is to say not in the ordinary course of very early development, are liable to be followed by attack in defence, and this attack in defence can very easily be mistaken for an instinctual impulse. Individuals may develop with this pattern of attack in defence replacing the pure instinctual impulse which belongs to the state of affairs following integration. In psycho-therapy where moments of integration can be extremely important, in an older child or even in an adult, the psycho-therapist needs to have a clear understanding of the work of integration and in practice it may be only for a brief period of time that there is a special need for the therapist to be between the repudiated external world and the newly integrated individual. If the therapist is able to act here at this moment in the same way that the mother is able to act at the beginning in the care of her normal baby then the paranoid pattern need not become organised and the individual has the opportunity to develop a true instinctual impulse, that is to say an impulse that has a biological basis and is not like the attack in defence, which is non-inherent and which has an anxiety as its basis.

This point has practical importance clinically when it becomes important to see in a particular case that a paranoid pattern, by which I mean the tendency to attack in defence, although pathological, has a positive element in it which is the attainment of momentary integration.

This seems to me to be very near the theory expressed by Lydia Jackson.*

---

* Jackson, Lydia: (1954) *Aggression and Its Interpretation.*

CHAPTER 3

DWELLING OF PSYCHE
IN BODY

BODY EXPERIENCE   H OW EASY IT IS to take for
granted the lodgement of the psyche
in the body and to forget that this again is
an achievement. It is an achievement which by no means falls to the lot
of all. Also in some the process is exaggerated, and forced by parents
who take a great pride in infantile gymnastics. Even those who seem to
live in the body may develop ideas of existing a little further out than the
skin, and the word ectoplasm seems to have been applied to the part of
the self that is not body-contained. By contrast, in hysteria, there may be
a condition in which the skin is not included in the personality and even
becomes bloodless and meaningless to the patient.

The skin is universally obviously important in the process of the
localisation of the psyche exactly in and within the body. Management
of the skin in infant care is an important factor in the promotion of a
healthy living in the body, in the same way that holding promotes
integration. Whereas a use of the intellectual processes detracts from the
attainment of a psyche–soma co-existence, the experience of functions
and of skin sensation and of muscle erotism helps towards this
attainment. It could be said of all human beings that at times when
instinctual frustrations lead to a feeling of hopelessness or futility the
fixing of the psyche in the body becomes loosened, and a period of
psyche and soma unrelatedness has to be endured. This can be
exaggerated to any degree in ill-health. The idea of a ghost, a disembod-
ied spirit, derives from this lack of essential anchoring of the psyche in
the soma, and the value of the ghost story lies in its drawing attention to
the precariousness of psyche–soma co-existence.

There is a direct application of theory here not only to the study and clinical management of skin disorders but also to the understanding of a large proportion of general psycho-somatic disorders. Psycho-somatic disorder is determined from many sources but the one that is usually omitted is perhaps the most important. It is common to see a discussion of the psychology of a psycho-somatic disorder with no mention of the positive value to the patient of the anchoring of some aspect of the psyche to some part of the body. There is psychotic anxiety underlying psycho-somatic disorder even although in many cases at more superficial levels there can be clearly shown to be hypochondriacal or neurotic factors.

There is no inherent identity of body and psyche. As we, the observers, see it, the body is essential to the psyche, which depends on brain functioning, and which arises as an organisation of the imaginative elaboration of body functioning. From the point of view of the developing individual, however, the self and the body are not inherently superimposed, the one on the other, and yet it is necessary for health that such a superimposition should become a fact, so that the individual can become able to afford to identify with what is, strictly speaking, not the self. The psyche gradually comes to terms with the body, so that in health there is eventually a state of affairs in which the body boundaries are also the psyche boundaries. The circle a 3-year-old child draws and calls "duck" is the duck's person as well as the duck's body. This is an achievement which is accompanied by the capacity to use the first pronoun. As is well known there are many who do not get so far or who lose what they have achieved.

Much of what was written about integration applies also to the dwelling of the psyche in the body. Quiet experiences and excited experiences each contribute in their own way. The two directions from which indwelling comes are the personal and the environmental; the personal experience of impulses, of skin sensations, of muscle erotism and of instinct involving excitement of the whole person, and also the matters of body management, and the meeting of instinctual demands, in such a way that gratification becomes possible. Particular stress can be laid here on physical exercise, especially that which comes spontaneously. It is accepted now, in child care, that it is valuable to allow for the tiny infant's pleasure in lying naked and kicking. The effect of swaddling has been studied as affecting personality development.*

The misfiring of instinctual experience can especially lead to a loosening or loss of the psyche–body bond. The relationship returns in time, however, provided there is good foundation of quiet (unexcited) management.

In adult psychiatry the term "depersonalisation" is used to describe the loss of relationship between psyche and soma. This term can be used to describe a common clinical state of normal children, a state that is commonly called a "bilious attack", although vomiting is not always a feature; the child is for a time flaccid, and pale as death, and is not available for contact – yet in a few minutes, or hours, the child comes round and is perfectly normal, with normal muscle tone and warm skin.

PARANOIA AND NAIVETÉ   It is sometimes instructive to contrast two extremes. In normal development integration and psyche–soma indwelling depend both on personal factors of living functional experience and on environmental care. Sometimes, however, the accent is on the former and sometimes it is on the latter.

In the former extreme type of development the individual infant is involved in an expectation of persecution. The gathering together of the self constitutes an act of hostility to the not-ME, and a return to rest is not a return to a resting place, because the place has been altered, and has become dangerous. Here is therefore a very early source of paranoid disposition, very early yet not inherited or truly constitutional.

In the latter extreme type of development the environmental care is the main cause of the gathering together of the self; indeed it could be said that the self has been gathered together. Here there is a relative absence of expected persecution, but instead there is basis for naiveté, for an inability to expect persecution, and for an irrevocable dependence on good environmental provision.

---

* Gorer, G. and Rickman, J. (1949): [*The People of Great Russia: A Psychological Study*].

In the normal, which is in between the two extremes, there is expectation of persecution, but also the experience of care as a protection from persecution.

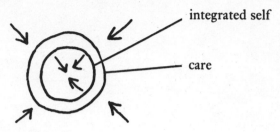

From this basis the individual can gradually become able to substitute self-care for care, and can therefore achieve a degree of independence that is not possible either in the naive or the paranoid extremes.

CHAPTER 4

THE EARLIEST STATES

DIAGRAM OF THE
ENVIRONMENT—
INDIVIDUAL SET-UP

IT IS POSSIBLE to examine a still earlier stage of individual development by once again employing a new method of presentation. We can make use of a diagram. The environment is now at its most important and cannot be left out either in theory or in practice.

Anything that is said now must be applicable to the infant just before birth at full term as well as after birth. It is not necessary for us to decide exactly at what age the foetus becomes a person to be studied psychologically but it can be said with fair certainty that whereas a post-mature child shows evidence of having been too long in the womb, a premature child shows evidence of having a poor capacity for experience as a human being. Undoubtedly the right time for an infant to be born from the psychological point of view is more or less the same as the right time from the physical angle, namely after nine months of intra-uterine existence.

The effect of the birth process will be studied in the next chapter, but here it is necessary to try to find a language applicable to the foetus near full term so that when we examine the effect of the birth trauma on the individual we can have something to work on, some way of looking at the human foetus which makes sense and which is not an imaginative construct on the part of the psychologist. The only question is: at what age does a human being begin to experience? An ability on the part of the baby before birth to retain body memories is something which must be allowed for, since there is a certain amount of evidence that from a date prior to birth nothing that a human being experiences is lost. It is well known that babies have certain movements in the womb which at first are rather like the swimming movements of a fish. The very valuable activities of infants are well known to mothers who look out for quickening at the sixth month; presumably sensations also start at some time or other; it is at any rate possible and indeed probable that there is a central organisation present which is ordinarily capable of noting these experiences.

I wish to postulate a state of being which is a fact in the ordinary baby before birth as well as afterwards. This state of being belongs to the infant and not to the observer. Continuity of being is health. If one takes the analogy of a bubble, one can say that if the pressure outside is adapted to the pressure inside, then the bubble has a *continuity of existence* and if it were a human baby this would be called "being". If on the other hand the pressure outside the bubble is greater or less than the pressure inside, then the bubble is engaged in a *reaction to impingement*. It changes in reaction to the environmental change, not from personal impulsive experience. In terms of the human animal this means that there is an interruption of being, and the place of being is taken by reaction to impingement. The impingement over, the reacting is no longer a fact, and there then is a return to being. This seems to me to be a statement which not only can take us back to intra-uterine life without demanding a stretch of imagination but which can also be brought forward and applied usefully as an extreme simplification of very complex phenomena belonging to later life at any age.

I. 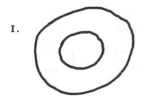 This represents the absolute isolation of the individual as part of the original unit of the environment–individual set-up.

The question arises: how will contact be made? Will it be as a part of the life process of the individual, or will it be as a part of the restlessness of the environment?

Let us say that active adaptation is nearly perfect. The result is

2.

then as in 2. The individual's own movements (perhaps an actual physical movement
of spine or leg in the womb) discover the
environment. This, repeated, becomes a
pattern of relationship.

In a less fortunate case the pattern of relationship is based on a
movement from the environment, as in 3. This merits the term

3.

impingement. The individual reacts to the
impingement, which is unpredictable since it
has nothing to do with the life process of the
individual. This, repeated, also becomes a
pattern of relationship, and the result is very

different from that of the first pattern. Whereas in the first the
aggregation of experiences feels like a part of life and real, in the second
the reaction to impingement detracts from the sense of real living,
which is only regained by return to isolation in quiet (4).

4.

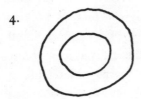

By this simple diagrammatic representation it can be shown that
environmental influences can start at a very early age to determine
whether a person will go out for experience or withdraw from the world
when seeking a reassurance that life is worth living. It is possible for a
mother's rigidity and unadaptability (due to her anxiety or her depression mood) to make itself evident in this way to her infant before the time
of birth.

Arguing from this postulate of being, continuity of being and
interruption of that continuity by reactions to impingement with return
to being, one can make a further statement: that from some time before

birth the human infant becomes accustomed to interruptions of continuity and begins to become able to allow for them provided they are not too severe or not too prolonged. In physical terms, this means that the baby has not only had experiences of change of pressure and of temperature and other simple environmental phenomena but also has appreciated them and begun to organise a way of dealing with them. From the observers' point of view the environment is just as important when there is a simple continuity of being as it is when it impinges and the continuity is interrupted by a reacting; for the infant, however, there is no reason for an awareness of the good enough environment. The good enough environment is absolutely essential, we must remember, for the natural development of the human being who is starting to live.

Attempts to study the psychology of the very early stages of human development have been marred and usually rendered useless by failure on the part of the psychologist to mention the good enough environment of which the infant is essentially unaware but without which the infant cannot develop. This consideration sometimes has a practical application even in an ordinary psycho-analytic treatment. As an example I would mention the case of a man patient who at a certain point in his analysis said while he was lying on the couch on his back:

"Just then I was curled up somewhere here in front of my face and I was twirling round and round."

Immediately I placed an environment around the curled-up infant, saying to the patient: "When you tell me that, you are also implying something which you could not know about, that is, the existence of what I would call a medium." (I was of course referring both to the physical condition in the womb and also to the psychological environment.) The patient said: "I see what you mean, like the oil in which a wheel revolves." (Analogy of gear box or crown wheel.)

As a result of my knowing what to do with this moment of withdrawal the experience turned into a very valuable regressive moment in the analysis, and led to big changes including the patient's ability to deal in a new way with external reality.

In all kinds of infant care and childhood management, as well as in the nursing of the physically and mentally sick, this simple diagram of a medium containing the individual is of value to the person representing the environment.

The essential principle is that by active adaptation to simple needs (instinct has not yet taken up its central position) the individual can BE and need not know of environment. Also, failures of adaptation bring about interruption of continuity of being, reaction to environmental impingement, and a state of affairs that cannot be productive. Primary narcissism, or the state *prior to* the acceptance of the fact of an environment, is the only state out of which environment can be created.

ACTION OF GRAVITY   There is an important subsidiary consideration which affects the management of small infants as well as that of very ill psychotic patients who have regressed either as part of the illness or in the course of the treatment on account of illness. I refer to the first experience of the action of gravity.

It is necessary to postulate a stage, which belongs to intra-uterine life, in which gravity has not yet appeared; love, or care, can only be expressed and appreciated in physical terms, in environmental adaptation which is applied from all directions. One of the changes brought about by the birth of the child is that the newborn infant has to adapt to something quite new, which is the experience of being pushed up from below instead of held all round. The infant changes from being loved from all directions to being loved from below only. Mothers appreciate this by the way they hold their babies and sometimes do them up tight in swaddling clothes; they try to give the baby time to get used to the new phenomenon. Clumsiness in regard to the management of this change from the pre-gravitational to the gravitational era gives a basis to the dream of falling for ever, or of being lifted up to infinite heights. It is clear from the symptomatology of older people that from the infant's point of view the change from the one era to the other can mean a change from being loved to being neglected.

CHAPTER 5

A PRIMARY STATE OF BEING:
PRE-PRIMITIVE STAGES

A T F I R S T there is unintegration, there is no bond between body and psyche, and no place for a not-ME reality. Theoretically this is the original state, unpatterned and unplanned. In practice this is not true, for the infant is being cared for, that is to say loved, which means physically loved. Adaptation to need is almost complete.

As we look towards the earliest roots of emotional development we see more and more dependence. At the earliest stage the dependence on environment is so complete that it is not valuable to think of the new individual human being as the unit. In this stage the unit is the *environment–individual set-up* (or whatever it can better be called) of which unit the new individual is only a part. At this very early stage it is not logical to think in terms of an individual, and this is not only because of the degree of dependence, and not only because the new individual has not yet the power to discern environment, but also because there is not yet an individual self there to discriminate between ME and not-ME.

When we look we see a mother and we see a baby developing in her womb, or held in her arms, or otherwise in her care. But if we look through the baby's eyes we have not yet reached a stage at which there is a place to see from. Yet the germ of all future development is there, and continuity of experience of being is essential to the future health of the baby who will be an individual.

What is the state of the human individual as the being emerges out of not being? What is the basis of human nature in terms of individual development? What is the fundamental state to which every individual, however old and with whatever experiences, can return in order to start again?

A statement of this condition must involve a paradox. At the start is an essential aloneness. At the same time this aloneness can only take place under maximum conditions of dependence. Here at the beginning the continuity of being of the new individual is without any awareness of the environment and of the love in the environment which is the name we give (at this stage) to active adaptation of such a kind and degree that continuity of being is not disturbed by reaction to impingement.

Except at the start there is never exactly reproduced this fundamental and inherent aloneness. Nevertheless throughout the life of an individual there continues a fundamental unalterable and inherent aloneness, along with which goes unawareness of the conditions that are essential to the state of aloneness.

The wish to get to this aloneness is interfered with by various anxieties and is hidden in the healthy person's ability to be alone in the care of a part of the self detailed off for self-nursing.

The state prior to that of aloneness is one of unaliveness, and the wish to be dead is commonly a disguised wish to be not yet alive. The experience of the first awakening gives the human individual the idea that there is a peaceful state of unaliveness that can be peacefully reached by an extreme of regression. Most of what is commonly said and felt about death is about this first state *before aliveness*, where aloneness is a fact and long before dependence is encountered. The life of an individual is an interval between two states of unaliveness. The first of these, out of which aliveness arises, colours ideas people have about the second death.

Freud spoke of the inorganic state from which each individual emerges and to which each returns, and from this idea he formulated his idea of the Life and Death Instincts. There is evidence of Freud's genius in his putting forward this obvious fact and implying that a truth lay hidden in it. Neither Freud's immediate use of the fact nor his development of a theory of the Life and Death Instincts from it carries conviction with me, and it will be more fruitful if those who wish to develop Freud's work at this point shall discard all except the original idea.

I wish to juxtapose two separate formulations, acknowledging the paradox; an observer can perceive that each individual human being emerges as organic matter out of inorganic matter, and in due time returns to the inorganic state. (Even this is not true altogether since the individual develops from the ovum which has a prehistory in all the ancestral ova fertilised since the original emergence of organic matter from inorganic several million million years ago); at the same time, from the point of view of the individual and of individual experience (which constitutes psychology) the emergence has been not from an inorganic state but from aloneness; this state arising before dependence can be recognised, dependence being on absolute dependability; this state being much prior to instinct, and still more removed from capacity for guilt. What could be more natural than that this state that has been experienced should be reclaimed in explanation of the unknowable death that comes after life?

There is no capacity of the infant (or foetus) to be concerned with death. There must be, however, a capacity in every infant for concern about the aloneness of pre-dependence since this has been experienced, and this idea is something that is not altered by uncertainty as to the date at which the human infant starts to be.

The recognition of this inherent human experience of predependent aloneness is of immense significance. Freud's later development of the theory of Life and Death Instincts introduces perceived death, the perceived distinction between organic and inorganic states, and even the idea of destructiveness, and at the same time Freud omits reference to the original dependence, double because not yet sensed, and to the gradual sensing and perception of dependence. In the end his theory becomes a false theory of the death that comes as an end to life, and also a theory of aggressiveness which is also false because it avoids two vitally important sources of aggression: that which is inherent in the primitive love impulse (at the pre-ruth stage, apart from reaction to frustration) and that which belongs to the interruption of the continuity of being by impingement that enforces reaction. The development of psycho-analytic theory to cover these (and probably other) early phenomena has perhaps made Freud's theory of Life and Death Instincts redundant, and Freud's own doubt about the validity of the theory seems to me to have become more important than the theory itself. It is always possible, however, that I have misunderstood Freud's true meaning.

If the sequence is to be found, aloneness, double dependence, instinctual impulse in a state prior to ruth, then concern and guilt, it seems not necessary to introduce a "Death Instinct". If on the other hand there is no aggressive element in the primitive love impulse, but only anger at frustration, and if therefore the change from ruthlessness to concern is of no importance, then it is necessary to look round for an alternative theory of aggression, and then the Death Instinct must be re-examined.

Death, for an infant at the beginning, means something quite definite, namely loss of being on account of prolonged reaction to environmental impingement (failure of good enough adaptation). There is no need to go beyond this, and to strain at a theory of an early infantile knowledge of unaliveness, which is absurd since it implies a great deal of development which, by hypothesis, has not yet taken place.

CHAPTER 6

CHAOS

I T IS NOT NECESSARY to postulate an original state of chaos. Chaos is a concept which carries with it the idea of order; and darkness too is not there at the beginning, since darkness implies light. At the beginning before each individual creates the world anew there is a simple state of being, and a dawning awareness of continuity of being and of continuity of existence in time.

Chaos first arrives in the history of the emotional development of the individual through reactive interruptions of being, especially when such interruptions last too long. Chaos is at first a broken line of being, and recovery occurs through re-experience of continuity; if the disturbance is beyond a degree that is tolerable according to earlier experiences of continuous being, then by crude economic laws a quantity of chaos enters into the individual's constitution.

Chaos becomes meaningful exactly as there is to be discerned some kind of order. It represents an alternative to order, and by the time chaos itself can be sensed by the individual it has already become a kind of order, a state which may become organised in defence against anxieties associated with order.

Chaos gathers to itself new meaning in relation to the order that is called integration. Unintegration, the primary state, is not chaotic. Disintegration is chaotic, being an alternative to order, and it can be said to be a crude kind of defensive organisation, defensive against the anxieties that integration brings. Nevertheless disintegration is not a state that of itself can go forward, and in so far as disintegration must be maintained, so far must emotional development be in abeyance. Each form of chaos contributes to the chaos that belongs to the subsequent stages, and recovery from chaos in an early stage gives a positive contribution to recovery from chaos later.

No doubt there is a degree of chaotic environment which can only result in a chaotic defensive state in the individual, with a result difficult to distinguish clinically from the mental defect that belongs to poverty of brain tissue. The defect results in this case from a permanent hold-up of development from a very early date.

The chaos of the inner world is a much later phenomenon. In the language of later phenomena, chaos in the inner world is an organised state that derives from oral sadism, and belongs to the instinctual life of the human being who has attained unit status, and has an inside and an outside. Hypochondriacal anxiety belongs to this chaos within, and depression (in one form) implies a magical control over all inner phenomena, pending reconstitution of orderliness within.

The chaos in the external world which is engineered by the depressive patient represents the individual's attempt to show what the inside is like. In defence against such a procedure the individual may become obsessed with the need for external orderliness, as in obsessional neurosis; but obsessional behaviour all the time points to chaos within, so that the obsessional orderliness cannot heal because it can only deal with the external representations or denials of the inner chaos.

First, then, there is no chaos because there is no order. This can be called unintegration. Chaos appears in relation to integration, and a return to chaos is called disintegration.

The next defensive states are not chaotic, but are of the nature of splitting. Splitting is an essential state in every human being, but one that need not be significant if the cushioning of illusion is made possible by the mother's management. In absence of active adaptation that is good enough the splitting becomes significant, with the following result:

A. Root of true self, with spontaneity, related omnipotently to subjective world, incommunicable, and

B. False self related on compliance basis (without spontaneity) to what we call external reality.

Gradually, as development proceeds, the individual can encompass the splitting that exists in the personality, and then lack of wholeness is called dissociation.

The attainment of unit status and of the depressive position makes possible the dramatisation of chaos, of splitting and of dissociations in the personal inner world, the complex results of personal instinctual experiences being incorporated into these dramatisations.

Disintegration after the individual has attained unit status is an organised undoing of integration, brought about and maintained because of intolerable anxiety in experience of wholeness. The splitting up in disintegration occurs along lines of cleavage in the inner world set-up, or of perceived outer world cleavage.

Dissociation is a term describing a condition of the relatively well developed personality, in which there is a rather exaggerated lack of communication between various elements. For instance there may be an absence of communication between the sleeping and waking states by remembered dreams. There is a normal dissociation (in time) between the life of a child of 3 and the life of that child after growing a few years older. Dissociation may show as a liability to "fugues", to periods of action and life that are out of character, and unremembered after.

The individual now becomes able to lose touch with the vast organisations associated with primitive levels of existence, and to enjoy a consciousness, enriched and also troubled by the unconscious. Certain elements in the self remain unacceptable to the self and a special form of unconscious (the repressed) is now a feature.

Repression is the term given to the loss from the consciousness of a more or less healthy person of groups of feelings, memories, and ideas, the cause being intolerable pain that belongs to consciousness of coincident love and hate, and of fear of retaliation. Allied to this is inhibition of instinct. It is in respect of repression that psycho–analysis brings about relief in the classical way, by enabling the patient to become conscious of the conflict and to tolerate the anxiety that belongs to a free instinctual expression.

If development proceeds well the individual becomes able to deceive, to lie, to compromise, to accept conflict as a fact and to abandon the extreme ideas of perfection and an opposite to perfection that make existence intolerable. Capacity for compromise is not a characteristic of the insane.

The mature human being is neither so nice nor so nasty as the immature. The water in the glass is muddy, but is not mud.

CHAPTER 7

THE INTELLECTUAL FUNCTION

A T FIRST there is soma, then a psyche that in health gradually becomes anchored to the soma; sooner or later a third phenomenon appears which is called intellect or mind.

The best approach to a study of the place of the mind in human nature is from the basis of simple psyche–soma existence, with environment that is good enough.

At first the environment must make 100% adaptation to need, otherwise the state of being is interrupted by reaction to impingement. Soon however a total adaptation is unnecessary, and a gradual maladaptation to need becomes a help (as well as being inevitable). The intellect has begun to explain and to allow for and to expect maladaptation (up to a certain amount) and thus to turn some degree of maladaptation back into total adaptation. Experiences are catalogued, classified and related to a time factor. Long before thinking becomes a feature, and thinking perhaps requires words, the intellect has had a function to perform. The intellectual function is therefore variable to a high degree, from infant to infant, since the work that needs to be done by the mind depends not on inherent factors of being and of growth so much as on the behaviour of the environment, or of the mother who is caring for the infant. Chaotic management (mother insane) causes intellectual muddle, and a type of mental defect, but a slight overstraining by maladaptation at the start can cause intellectual overgrowth, and mind development that can be used later in a valuable way, although this condition carries with it some degree of instability since as a phenomenon it is reactive rather than inherent.

In one extreme type of case an intellectual overgrowth that is successful in accounting for maladaptation to need becomes of itself so important in the child's economy that it (the mind) becomes the nursemaid that acts as mother-substitute and cares for the baby in the child's self. The mind in such a case has a false function and a life of its own, and it dominates the psyche–soma instead of being a special function of the psyche–soma. The result may be gratifying to teachers and parents who like cleverness. Nevertheless the psychiatrist knows also of the dangers and of the unrealness of everything to an individual who has developed in such a way. This approach to the study of the use of the mind must be put alongside the study of intellectual capacity which depends on the quality of brain, a quality that is largely a matter of inheritance. It is this latter quality of the intellect which it is intended to examine in the routine intelligence tests that have been carefully and ingeniously devised in recent years. These tests form no basis, however, for the assessment of a personality or of personal emotional growth.

CHAPTER 8

WITHDRAWAL AND REGRESSION

I N THE FINAL STAGES of a psycho-therapy in which there has been regression localised to the analytic situation, and developed and held within the professional setting of the treatment, it becomes evident that there is a close relationship between this regression and the ordinary withdrawal. Withdrawal is a common phenomenon, and if conditions are not favourable the withdrawal is organised in a hostile way, and the word sulking is applicable.

It is helpful to think of withdrawal as a condition in which the person concerned (child or adult) holds a regressed part of the self and nurses it, at the expense of external relationships.

If, at the moment of withdrawal in a psycho-therapy where there is opportunity for delicate observation and management, the therapist quickly steps in and holds the baby, then the person hands over the nursing to the therapist and slips over into becoming the infant.

Withdrawal is a protective procedure, and is useful, but return from withdrawal brings no relief and indeed there are complications inherent in the process of return from withdrawal. Regression has however a healing quality, since early experiences can be corrected in a regression and there is a true restfulness in the experience and acknowledgement of dependence. Return from regression depends on a regaining of independence, and if this is well managed by the therapist the result is that the person is in a better state than before the episode. All this depends of course on the existence of a capacity for trust, as well as on the therapist's capacity to justify trust, and there may be a long preliminary phase of treatment concerned with the building up of confidence.

In regression in a psycho-therapy the patient (of whatever age) must be able to come eventually to an unawareness of environmental care and of dependence, which means that the therapist is giving a good enough adaptation to need. Here is a state of primary narcissism, which must be reached at certain moments in the treatment. On the return journey the patient needs the therapist in two roles – the worst imaginable, in all respects, and the best – or an idealised mother-figure engaged in perfect child care. Gradual recognition of the identity of the idealised and the very bad therapists goes hand in hand with gradual acceptance on the part of the patient of the good and the bad in the self, of the hopelessness and of that which is hopeful, of the unreal with the real, indeed of all the contrasting extremes. At the end, if all goes well, there is a person who is human and imperfect related to a therapist who is imperfect in the sense of being unwilling to act perfectly beyond a certain degree and beyond a certain length of time.

These same things belong to ordinary infant care, but they are less easy to study by direct observation of the mother and infant than by the study of the therapeutic situation.

CHAPTER 9

THE BIRTH EXPERIENCE

I T CAN CERTAINLY be claimed that there is no exact know-ledge about the effect of the birth process on the infant that is being born. It is even difficult to prove that there is any effect at all. Many would argue that there can be no effect since the infant is not yet there as a human being to be affected. The point of view that I am putting forward here is that, at full term, there is already a human being in the womb, one that is capable of having experiences and of accumulating body memories and even of organising defensive measures to deal with traumata (such as the interruption of continuity of being by reaction to the impingements from the environment in so far as it fails to adapt).

According to this view foetuses at full term come to the birth process each with an individual capacity or lack of capacity for dealing with the great changeover from being unborn to born. In this setting it must be remembered that there is an extreme variability in the degree to which the event of birth is traumatic to the infant, assuming that the infant is there as something to be reckoned with.

I find it necessary to postulate a normal birth, that is to say a changeover from the state of being unborn to being born that is not traumatic.

The question is: what does this word mean in terms of the psychology of the infant? Normal birth involves three main features: firstly, that the infant experiences a gross interruption of the conti-nuity of being (by impingement of altered pressure, etc.), but has already become to a sufficient degree capable of bridging the gaps in continuity of being associated with reaction to impingement. The second is that the infant has built up memories of sensations and impulses that are self phenomena since they belong to the periods in which being rather than reacting was the order of the moment. The third feature is that the mechanics of the birth process are not too abnormal, that is to say that the birth is neither precipitate nor prolonged. On these three assumptions it is possible to conceive of a birth in which, from the infant's point of view, the change from the unborn to the born state is brought about *by the infant*, who is biologically ready for the changes and who would be adversely affected by their delay. By this I mean that the infant has a series of impulses and that the progression towards being born comes within the infant's capacity to feel responsible. We know of course that the birth was brought about by the uterine contractions. It was the infant's impulse *from the infant's point of view* that produced the changes and the physical progression, usually head first, towards an unknown and new position. Certainly it would come within the normal that there should be a considerable degree of reaction to the various new impinging sensations so that there must inevitably be repeated interruptions of the continuity of being, straining to the utmost the infant's capacity to allow for these interruptions. It is necessary to start with the assumption that there can be a birth which from the infant's point of view is not to an excessive degree an impingement, but is something produced by the impulses towards movement and change that spring directly out of the infant's aliveness. The change in the infant's state from not breathing to breathing is usually brought forward as an example of the essentially traumatic nature of being born or of having been born.

I suggest, however, that the normal infant's previous experience of recovery from reacting to impingements, plus the infant's biological readiness for the changeover to actual breathing, can cover even the initiation of breathing, and in fact that a post-mature infant can be already at birth suffering from a delay in breathing. Similarly a premature infant may lose something of the *value* of the birth experience.

The baby born by Caesarian section is a special case and the study of the pattern of anxiety in persons born by Caesarian section might easily provide interesting side-lights on the problem of the meaning of birth to the infant, as Freud himself suggested.*

I assume that in a normal birth there is neither haste nor delay, and that the baby born by Caesarian section, while better off than other infants in some respects, has lost something through being deprived of the ordinary birth experience. The most important variable factor is the delay that is so frequent in the birth process owing to the fact that mothers start having babies rather late in our culture; this, coupled with the inhibitions that belong to civilisation, and with the fact of the largeness of the human baby's head, brings about a state of affairs in which it is unlikely that many normal births do in fact take place. Slight degrees of delay beyond the capacity of the infant to tolerate the delay must be very common, and clinically one finds here a basis for an intellectual interest in time, and in the parcelling up of time, and in the development of a timing sense. Many human beings carry body memories of the birth process as a striking example of delay beyond comprehension, since for an infant reacting to the impingement of a delayed birth there is no precedent and no yardstick by which to measure the delay or to predict the outcome. There is no way of letting a baby know during a delayed birth that half an hour or so will see the matter through, and for this reason the baby is caught up in indefinite or "infinite" delay. This sort of painful experience gives a powerful basis for such a matter as form in music, where without rigidity of framework the idea of the end is kept before the listener from the beginning. Formless music is boring. Formlessness is infinitely boring for those who are particularly concerned with this type of anxiety on account of delays just beyond comprehension that occurred in their infancy. Music with a clear form structure brings its own reassurance apart altogether from the other values in the music.

This is a rather sophisticated example and there are many who cannot achieve using form for reassurance against infinity. For them a crude statement of an exact programme according to the clock is necessary unless boredom is to overtake them. Infinity of delay

---

* Personal communication [from Freud] to John Rickman.
[See also Freud (1905).]

belongs rather naturally to the birth process when it is not quite normal and it is especially important to certain infants that they are able to work out the probabilities with their minds so that they can become able to predict a feed by the sounds in the kitchen or to account for delay eventually by an understanding of the sort of reasons that make mothers unpunctual.

In the birth process there is the major change from not breathing to breathing. I have evidence derived from clinical work that the baby may become aware of the breathing of the mother in the sense of belly movements or rhythmical changes of pressure or sounds, and that after birth the baby can be needing to re-establish contact with the mother's physiological functioning, especially her breathing. For this reason I think it probable that some infants must be allowed naked contact with the mother and especially to be able to be moved by her moving belly. It is likely that for the infant who is just born it is the breathing of the mother that is meaningful, while the rapid breathing of the infant is meaningless until it begins to approach the frequency of the mother's breathing rhythm. Certainly infants, without knowledge of what they are doing, play about with rhythms and cross-rhythms, and careful observation can sometimes show infants to be working in their breathing rate with their heart rate (for instance, breathing in and out to the accompaniment of four heart-beats). A little later they can be found dealing with the difference between their breathing rate and that of their mothers, and perhaps with relationships based at first on breathing at double or treble frequency.

The sequence may be this: the infant's intra-uterine awareness of mother's breathing; infant's extra-uterine awareness of mother's breathing; infant's awareness of own breathing. No doubt if in a particular case there is no special reason for breathing awareness then physiology just takes over, and the child breathes and becomes aware of breathing without there being anything more interesting to be said; but this would not necessarily be the normal. It would belong particularly to the development of the mental defective. But as there are all types of human being it may be that there are many infants for whom breathing is not really a very important thing because they have other interests with prior claim, such as for instance eidetic imagery or the equivalent to this in the auditory or kinaesthetic fields.

Abnormal birth from the infant's point of view means, from our point of view, prolonged labour. Most of the various complications which we know about as adult observers must mean nothing to the infant being born. We have evidence however that what the infant perceives is being catalogued except in so far as delays and perhaps the pains of constriction disturb too much or obtain for so long a period that the continuity of being is broken. Apart from a liability of the newborn infant to convulsive attack caused by cortical bruising there may be "blackouts" as one might call them, without physical basis. The possibility that they can provide a pattern for the development of "absences" at a later stage must be borne in mind. It appears that only a certain amount of birth trauma can be encompassed as experience by the infant, and that the worst belongs not to the severe disturbance producing unconsciousness so much as to a tantalising situation in which there is repeated progression without too much pressure and yet with oft-repeated lack of outcome.

It follows that if this, or some of this, be true, then there is a very real meaning to the word normal as a description of a newly born child.

Certainly most babies are not in quite a normal state at birth and they need an exaggeration of the early management techniques whereby the mother provides an environment as nearly as possible reproducing the intra-uterine condition. There appears to be an ordinary need for being held quietly after birth. It is likely that not only is the skin very sensitive to changes of texture and temperature but also the same statement can be made in general psychological terms.

It is probable that in careful nursing techniques the infant who has been through a specially tantalising labour needs to be allowed immediately after birth a prolonged period of the very simplest possible state, either of being held or of its nearest available equivalent. Certainly the idea of taking a newborn baby and subjecting the baby to cleaning and even bathing cannot be a suitable procedure in all cases. Many babies need a period in which to recover poise, as it were, or to recover a sense of continuity of being rather than of reaction to impingement, so that they can begin again to have impulses and to be even reaching out for feeds. It is valuable to the mother that she should see her baby and even feel the baby against her body immediately after birth, and some mothers feel that this is so important that twilight sleep is intolerable to them unless they can recover from it immediately the baby is born. It would be inaccurate, however, to say that *all* babies are ready for their mothers immediately after birth, since many have had experiences from which they need to recover. It is perhaps not sufficiently recognised that both the mother and the baby who is not too disturbed can each get a great deal from a few moments together with the baby in contact by skin to skin and perhaps moved by the mother's breathing. There may be no question of an immediate interest in feeding, although there seems to be room for every possible kind of variation within the term normal.

The disturbance of the infant which may result from the birth experience cannot, I suggest, be thought of simply in terms of the tearing of the meninges and of haemorrhage into the spinal canal. These physical traumata occur with considerable frequency and sometimes the physical state dominates the scene, but in the normal case there is not so much physical trauma that the emotional needs of the mother and the baby must be over-ridden.

Perhaps the best evidence that the birth experience is a real experience, or in other words that the infant is already there at that time to have experiences, comes from the very great pleasure that nearly all children get (and adults too for that matter) from activities and games which involve an acting out of some or other aspect of the birth process. In this way again it can be seen that in so far as the birth process is normal it has value for the infant, so that an infant born under heavy narcosis on account of the anaesthetising of the mother can be said to have missed something.

There are those who find evidence of body memories belonging to the birth process and who yet do not believe that there is an individual present at the time of birth capable of having an experience. These do sometimes try to find a way out of the dilemma by postulating a racial unconscious, a sort of inherited memory of birth arising out of the fact

of innumerable births of ancestors. But the theory of the racial unconscious can only too easily be used as a side-tracking of the very
interesting and important phenomenon of the development of the
individual, and the memory of personal experiences.

It is not certain whether Freud himself believed that each person
retains body memories of the personal birth process, or whether he
assumed something like a racial unconscious, when he made the
observation that the pattern of anxiety might be determined (at any
rate in part) by the individual's birth experiences. Possibly he believed
in a racial memory at first but later tended to think more in terms of the
individual's own history.

It is fairly obvious that if infants are capable, in the way that I am
assuming, of having experiences at this early age, then when there are
delays in the birth process there can be very uncomfortable breathing
sensations, especially when there is pressure on the cord or when the
cord is round the neck; so that the baby becomes partially asphyxiated
before being in a position to breathe.

These considerations, although difficult, prepare the way for a
consideration of results of careful history-taking. Histories taken in a
proper way from mothers who still have the facts in their possession
show that (quite apart from bodily disturbances) infants vary in regard
to their capacity to begin an instinctual life in terms of breast feeding.
The variations in the mother's capacity to feed, dependent on her own
psychology, her own history, and the physical state of her breasts and
nipples, can be taken fully into account, and yet two infants are hardly
like each other in their state when the mother and the baby at length
begin to make relationship. We must reserve the word normal for the
infant who is ready if the mother is ready, and then we can use the
word abnormal to describe all the degrees of irritability which we find
and which often make it impossible for a mother to feed one particular
baby although she has had no difficulty with her others.

It is as if some babies are born paranoid, by which I mean in a state
of expecting persecution, whereas others are not. It is very easy to
claim that the paranoid babies have inherited a tendency or are
showing a constitutional factor, but the arguments along these lines
must be preceded by a study of the prehistory of the infant taking into

full account the limitations belonging to the infant's immaturity. I have described ways in which a paranoid disposition can be congenital but not inherited.

For those who do not believe that there is a human being present at this early stage, then there is no alternative but to accept the constitutional factor, since there can be no doubt that some babies are very "difficult" from the beginning.

In published accounts of psycho-analytic theory, which was based at first on the study of neurosis in adults, it would often seem as if life starts for the infant with the first feed. This is most certainly not true and any study is welcome which throws light on the nature of the infant at the time of the first feed, and also at the time of being born. It is not necessary for everything to be known all at once. The question is: what is the best approach to the study of this subject? The obvious answer is: a direct observation of infants. There are very big difficulties here, however, since it is not possible to observe an infant except in the sense of looking at the body and watching behaviour. Probably the most convincing study of the needs of very early infancy comes from the observations on analytic patients who have regressed in the course of psycho-analytic treatment. In regard to my own experience, that which has taught me most has been the observation of steady regression followed by progression in borderline cases, that is to say in individuals who must reach to illness of psychotic type in themselves in the course of treatment. The more severely ill patients, those who have broken down into regressive types of illness apart altogether from psycho-therapy, are not so helpful in this work; but from the work of Rosen it is possible to see that a direct application of the principles that have been found to work in the treatment of less ill persons can produce results with even degenerated mental hospital patients. Even if Rosen's results were not lasting they would be sufficient to prove that the study of psychosis is the same as the study of the very early psychological history of the developing individual.

If this is put the other way round, it is the study of the early stages of individual emotional development that can provide the clue to mental health in respect of freedom from psychosis. There is therefore no more important study than that of the individual at the beginning intimately involved with the environment. Here meet the several disciplines of general scientific enquiry, of psychiatric and psycho-therapeutic diagnosis and management, and also of philosophy, to which we owe the courage to proceed step by step towards a better understanding of human nature.

CHAPTER 10

ENVIRONMENT

I T IS NOW POSSIBLE to make a study of environment.
In *maturity* environment is something to which the individual contributes and for which the individual man or woman takes responsibility. In a community in which there is a sufficiently high proportion of mature individuals there is a state of affairs which provides the basis for what is called democracy. If the proportion of mature individuals is below a certain number, democracy is not something which can become a political fact since affairs will be swayed by the immature, that is to say, by those who by identification with the community lose their own individuality or by those who never achieve more than the attitude of the individual dependent upon society.

In observing the *adolescent* we see the gradual widening of the group with which the individual can identify without loss of personal identity. The basis of the group is the home life and we know how convenient it is for the adolescent if the original home continues to exist so that it can be rebelled against as well as used, and so that there can be an experimentation with other and with wider groupings without loss of the original grouping which has a pre-history, that is to say, which existed in the formative early years before the latency period. Children in the *latency period* are greatly disturbed by the break-up of the home because at that time they should not be concerned with these matters; they need to be able to take the environment for granted and to be enriching themselves educationally and culturally and in play and in all types of personal experience.

There is a very special importance in the existence of the home situation for the boy and girl during the very important period of emotional growth *before the latency period* and after the achievement of the capacity for interpersonal relationships as between whole people. Where the family situation has as its basis a satisfactory union between the parents, then the small child is able to work out all the varying aspects of the triangular situation: instincts can be allowed their full development, both the heterosexual and the homosexual dream can be dreamed, and the full extent of the capacity for hate as well as for pure aggressiveness and for cruelty can become accepted by the individual child. All these things come about in the course of time because of the survival of the home and of the union between the parents, because of the arrival and survival and sometimes the illness or death of siblings, and because of the parents' capacity to distinguish between reality and dream.

While the existence of the home environment is very important at this stage it is not, however, essential. Perhaps it would be better to say that it gradually becomes less essential as time goes on and as the child becomes able to use substitute triangular situations in which to play out and work out the full extent of the feelings of which he or she is capable. It can be said that once a child has reached the capacity for interpersonal relationships in terms of whole persons then, if the family situation breaks, the child may still be able to manage if some substitute for the home is provided and a muddle is avoided. The death of parents is easier for children to stand or to recover from than the complications arising out of emotional difficulties between the parents. It may be said that the break-up of a home must distort the emotional development of a boy or girl in the pre-latency period but a great deal depends on the previous emotional development of the child. The type of disturbance is of this order, that for instance an older child may take over the mothering of a baby when the home breaks and may do well, but at a cost, since so great a responsibility ought not to have fallen on such young shoulders. Nevertheless the child remains a child and can even be enriched in some respects by the responsibilities. It is at this period that the child is only just becoming able to deal with separations from the parents and it is important to distinguish between those separations which imply the use of substitute triangular situations – going to stay with an aunt, for instance – and those which imply taking the child from known triangular situations into impersonal management, as for instance when it is necessary for a child to go into hospital. At this age the child has not only incorporated environmental patterns but has also built up a personal pattern of expectation; it has been aptly remarked that gradually the child develops an "internal environment", and this, as time goes on and growth takes place, makes for toleration of environmental failure and the organisation and production, in a positive way, of the emotional surroundings that the child desires. It is also important to remember that when a child becomes able to enjoy substitute triangular situations it is then the time to supply an opportunity for the exercise of the new capacity. The basis of the child's life continues to be the original triangular situation, the one in which the child is related to the two parents. It may be taken that the child of 2 is only insecurely started on this era in which substitute triangular situations can be used and a child of this age is certainly not ready to deal with the removal from known triangular situations into impersonal management.

The basis for daily visiting of children who have to be in a hospital, something which has become a common procedure only in recent years in this country, is this need of the small child for the simplified emotional environment. It can be said that the child of 2 who has developed well through the complexities of earlier emotional development is not ready to deal with impersonal care, and good physical care in a hospital is not sufficient; so that either the parents must maintain their relationship while the child is in hospital or else the child must have the opportunity to develop a substitute triangle of relationships in the institution which has unfortunately become necessary on account of some physical disability needing skilled treatment.

Without attempting to be exact about ages one can see that by the age of 5 many children are becoming able to make use of experiences away from home whereas at the age of 2 a child must be harmed by a break with the home situation, which means the simple state of affairs the basis of which is the union of the parents.

At an *earlier age*, and again I need not be exact, it is necessary to think of the environment while the child is consolidating the achievement of the depressive position in emotional development. As we go earlier, so we find the environment becoming more and more important. Already when the child is 2 and is normal and is working out the complexities of the relationship with the two parents, we find that the environment must be good enough and must be maintained. When we go earlier and think of the depressive position we know that the infant *cannot make the grade* without the continuous care of one person. It is now a question of the baby and the mother or the mother-substitute. The mother must be available to hold the situation in time; not only must she be available herself in a physical way but she must be well enough to be consistent in her attitude over a period of time, and she must survive the day and the collection of days that we call weeks and months in order that the infant may repeatedly experience the anxieties associated with the instinctual impulses, and the working-through after these experiences and the renewal of a relationship with the mother after the period of working-through. Babies can survive when no one plays this role but they survive with something missing in their emotional development, something which is of vital importance, and the result is a restlessness and a lack of capacity for concern, a lack of depth, and an incapacity for constructive play and eventually an inability to work; with a result that is unsatisfactory both to the individual and to society.

The special function of the mother or mother-substitute *in introducing the infant to the external world* and in making possible the illusion of contact has been described. It could be said that this aspect of mother-care is not so specifically a function of the actual mother since if it is successful the infant has a capacity which can be used for life, whereas by contrast in the matter of the depressive position it is the capacity to make reparation, at first to the mother herself, that is important. Nevertheless it would appear that the very sensitive adaptation to need which is required in order that the infant shall make a good start in this matter of contact with external reality necessitates a state of affairs which is not likely to be present unless it is the actual mother who has the baby in her care.

At the beginning the degree of adaptation that is needed is so great that it can only be done well enough by someone who has had that sort of preparation for the task which is brought about naturally by the nine months of pregnancy, during which time the mother gradually becomes able to make an identification with the infant to a degree which is not possible even by the same mother a few weeks after the baby has been born.

In an examination of the factors leading to integration and to the indwelling of the psyche in the body, one of these concerns the environment and general physical care as an expression of love. It is here if at all that the technique rather than a personal relationship is important, so that in these matters there is a relatively smaller necessity for the mother to be the person in charge. In other words, if the technique of infant care is good, the matter of who it is that employs the technique is not so important. On the other hand it must be remembered that the experience of several techniques presents a confusing situation for the infant; it could be said that one person's technique is variable enough and about as much as an infant can stand in the very early stages without confusion being caused. A baby brought up in an institution can fare better in respect of integration and the indwelling of the psyche in the body than in respect of the initiation of contact with reality, and as I have pointed out, cannot fare well at all in the matter of the development of concern. The various aspects of emotional development are, however, so closely bound up with each other that it is very artificial to separate these matters out from each other.

To go *further back*, one becomes involved in the state of affairs in which the individual has no sense of time, no continuity of integration even if integration occurs at certain moments, and no capacity for feeling dependent. Also the intellectual capacity which gives understanding of adaptive failure has not yet developed and relief afforded by the imaginative elaboration which is the psyche aspect of function is not yet available. In these early stages tremendous forces are at work but the main comment should be that what forces exist are of great importance because of the fact of there being as yet no relief from the primitive crudities; simple economic factors reign, and if certain conditions are not present then certain distortions must occur. As we go back to the earliest stages we go towards the complete merging of the individual in the environment, that which is implied in the words primary narcissism. There is an intermediate state between this and interpersonal relationships which has very great importance, of which it could be said that between the mother who is physically holding the baby and the baby there is a layer which we have to acknowledge which is an aspect of herself and at the same time an aspect of the baby. It is mad to hold this view and yet the view must be maintained. There is a close analogy here with the physical situation prior to birth; the mother has a baby inside her. The womb has within it a whole organisation developed out of the individual ovum that has been fertilised. The endometrium has specialised to become intermingled with the placenta. Between the mother and the infant therefore is the amniotic sac and the placenta and the endometrium. There is no need for the analogy to be taken too far, but physically it is also true to say that there is a set of substances between the mother and the baby which is absolutely essential until separation eventually occurs. This set of substances is then lost both to the mother and to the infant. In this stage which is so difficult to describe we as observers can easily understand where the mother ends and the infant begins. In the psychology of the individual, however, there is an important aspect of relationships in which it can be said that in the most intimate contact there is a lack of contact so that essentially each individual retains absolute isolation always and for ever. In the physical analogy it is true that the ovum was a lodger in the mother's body, not part of the mother, and after fertilisation there was a gradual organisation of the establishment of independence; biologically it can be said that the mother lost nothing of herself when the baby was born except that part of the endometrium which became intermingled with the placenta.

I have used the word mad, and purposely, because in the theory of the developing human being there is a double claim on this intermediate substance at the point of development from primary narcissism to object relationship. After the baby is born this substance that joins and also separates becomes represented by objects and phenomena of which it can be said once again that while they are part of the infant they are also part of the environment. Only gradually do we demand of the developing individual that there shall be a fully acknowledged distinction between external reality and inner psychic reality; indeed there is a relic of the intermediate substance in the cultural life of grown men and women, in fact in that which most clearly distinguishes human beings from the animals (religion, art, philosophy).

Prior to all this there is a state of *primary narcissism* or the state in which what we see as the infant's environment and what we see as the infant constitute together a unit. The clumsy term "environment–individual set-up" can be used here. The environment as we know it need not be mentioned because the individual has no means of perceiving it and indeed the individual is not there yet, not yet separated from the environmental aspect of the total unit. It is an achievement of healthy emotional development when the centre of gravity of being gradually shifts to the part of the total unit that we (the onlookers) can so easily see to be the infant.

At this very early stage it must be postulated that 100% adaptation of a physical kind must be supplied by the environment if healthy growth is to start and if the centre of gravity of being is to tend to be away from the surroundings and towards the centre where the foetus is. The mother, physically, takes over the environmental aspect of the total set-up.

An attempt has been made to describe the environmental factor relative to the various stages of emotional development. For a full understanding, however, it must be remembered that the *early stages are never truly abandoned*, so that in a study of the individual of whatever age all the primitive as well as the later types of environmental requirements will be found; and in child care as well as in psycho-therapy it is necessary all the time to be watching for the emotional age *at the moment* in order that the appropriate emotional environment can be provided.

When we watch the emotional development of the infant at these very early stages we feel how precarious it all is. Fortunately most of the environmental care is in physical terms; at the beginning it is instinctual and the mother's specialised orientation makes it likely that the important things happen apart altogether from understanding and knowledge, unless the mother is ill. It is to be noted, however, that a *return to an earlier stage of dependence* means pain and a sense of the precariousness that belongs to dependence. Presumably this is not a feature in the original development that proceeds normally. In illness or in the course of psycho-therapy regression may occur, and regression to infancy states can have a healing quality provided that the very intense suffering associated with dependence experienced regressively can be tolerated. The clumsiness of the psycho-therapist as compared with the mother makes it inconceivable that regression to dependence even in a carefully controlled treatment is pleasurable.

The idea of a wonderful time in the womb (the oceanic feeling, etc.) is a complex organisation of denial of dependence. Any pleasure that comes with regression belongs to the idea of a perfect environment, and against this has to be weighed the idea, just as real for the regressed child or adult, of an environment so bad that there can be no hope of a personal existence.

CHAPTER 11

Psycho–somatic disorder reconsidered

T HE THEORY OF psycho-somatic disorder can now be reviewed. In the consideration of a psycho-somatic disorder it is necessary to have in mind the whole of what is known of the emotional development of the individual, and to work out the relationship between the physical and the psychological elements bit by bit. I could best describe this process by taking a few examples.

ASTHMA   (a) There is a biochemical factor in some asthma cases, the operation of which is obscure, and the word allergy does not take us further except in the suggestion that it carries with it that there is a sensitivity on the part of the individual to certain proteins. In some cases it would appear that this, the physical side of the condition, is the important one, at least in the initial stages. If it be assumed that in one case the cause is physical, then there is quickly added a secondary psychological overlay which is variable according to the individual. It is not possible to have asthma without being altered by having it and by being liable to it.

(b) In various studies it has been shown that asthma is associated with an environmental factor. It is usually claimed that over-mothering predisposes to asthma as well as to several other kinds of symptom. If these investigations are correct there is something to be said about the theory which is important, which is that the continuing adverse external factor is not necessarily the original cause; and the original cause may or may not be an over-mothering at some specific and important early date. In any case in a full understanding of asthma with a powerful external adverse factor it is necessary to understand the impact on the individual child of the repressed unconscious that underlies the mother's compulsion towards over-mothering. This must be variable. In regard to the child considered as a whole person concerned in interpersonal relationships asthma is sometimes quite clearly related to phases of extra strain such as the birth of a new child or episodes in which there is imposed on the child an emotional burden which the child cannot at the time bear, whereas another child might develop enuresis or some other manifestation of distress; asthma turns up for reasons associated with deeper factors, some of which are known and some of which are not known.

An analysis of a child with asthma, if the analyst keeps to the level of interpersonal relationships and the conflict between love and hate, reveals a great deal that is of value. The child develops insight and becomes able to allow for the asthma or even to avoid it by adopting certain procedures. Nevertheless analysis of an asthmatic which keeps to these levels may or may not succeed in respect of asthma symptoms, although it may well succeed in enabling the child to develop both in character and personality and in a general freedom of relationships. Analysis at this level never reveals the nature of the asthma itself. In a treatment which takes into consideration the special point in the development of the relationship between the infant and the mother which has been called the depressive position in emotional development a great deal more light is thrown on the meaning of asthma to the child. There may be rich fantasy systems about the inside of the chest and all kinds of variations on the theme of the chest standing for the belly or the chest as an alternative to the belly or the general interior of the psyche which has become a unit. The management of fierce internal battles and the control of the forces of good and evil within the self – these and all the other phenomena contributing to hypochondriacal anxiety are found and are valuable when conscious in the child instead of unavailable, and are valuable to us in our attempt to understand.

There is still no clue, however, to the nature of asthma. In the analysis in which there is regression to greater dependence and in the analytic situation and in the transference relationship, the patient is infantile at certain times or over certain phases. There is a more near approach to the real nature of the asthma itself, although it must be admitted that much remains for understanding. The infant state brings with it a reliving of breathing problems associated with the beginning of after-birth and with the birth process itself. Body memories of very great importance appear and physical disturbances of the breathing apparatus turn up in the treatment session which had not been available previously as memory material even in dreams. The clue to asthma is still, however, missing, since these body memories of respiratory difficulties need not lead to asthma and may be associated instead with a liability to bronchitis and with all kinds of other respiratory disorders and sensations of choking, etc. It is not until the treatment arrives at very early stages in the emotional development of the individual that the asthma seems to begin to fit into place, as for instance when the patient is concerned with the establishment of a true self as the place from which to live and the settlement of this true self in the body. It is here that the philological link between the word soul and the word breath becomes sensible. The to and fro of the breathing is found to be intolerable in the case of certain anxieties associated with the escape of the true and perhaps hidden self, and in screaming as well as in asthma one gets the conflict between the need for a free ingress and egress and anxiety about a lack of control over what comes in and goes out of the newly established psyche unit. The well-known relationship between infantile eczema and asthma is not understood in psychological terms, and until this is done the argument in favour of a common physical basis for the two conditions must be allowed.

In this brief review of asthma I have attempted more to illustrate the use of the psychology of the various kinds and layers rather than to make a complete statement of the subject of the psychology of asthma.

GASTRIC ULCER   If we examine the subject of gastric ulcer we can again use the same system. The purely physical causes of gastric ulcer need not be discussed. In terms of environment it can be shown that conditions leading to continued emotional stress are present in a significant proportion of gastric ulcer cases. In some of these the removal of the adverse external factor is an important part of the physical treatment, and the treatment must be physical because there is a physical and dangerous lesion. In treatment by hospitalisation and, for instance, a diet of milk only, given in frequent small quantities, it must be remembered that there is also a separation of the patient from the home surroundings and a justification for release from anxieties associated with work. If these anxieties are not dealt with by management the treatment by physical means is liable to fail; the patient's confidence in the doctor and in the nurse is of supreme importance as a part of the management and in the displacement of continuing adverse emotional factors that belong to the patient's life. Incidentally, the treatment may involve an interruption of opportunity for various indulgences which of course have a psychological cause.

In terms of interpersonal relationships as between whole people there is much to be found if a search is made. The whole range of fantasy and dream is available and the various cross-identifications are found on investigation. An analysis of a patient at this level may allay anxieties and enable the patient to become able to cope with environmental factors by relieving him or her of the need to relive unfortunate early experiences which had become forgotten. Analysis in terms of the depressive position reveals a great deal in these cases, particularly a defensive mood of a chronic kind with depression hidden at the core. This is called common anxious restlessness in childhood or hypomania, and in psycho-analytic theory the restlessness is thought of as a manic defence against depression; a constant over-activity and bolstering up excitement leads to physiological alterations which can easily affect such things as the acidity of the stomach contents. A source is also found here for the various compulsive indulgences and for certain minor disturbances such as quick eating and unwise choice of foods. It is not any one of these things that leads to gastric ulcer but the operation of a number of factors over a period of time. Analysis of a patient of this kind is different according to whether the ulcer is present or whether the conditions only are there which could easily lead to the formation of chronic ulceration. In the former case the ulcer will be given significance by the patient according to the fantasies available about the inner world phenomena. In a proportion of cases the core of the illness will be found to be the depression which underlies the hypomanic mood, in spite of the fact that great relief was obtained by the analysis in terms of conflict between the love and hate and interpersonal relationships and the anxieties inherent in the Oedipus Complex. There is no particular reason to expect analysis of the more primitive aspects to contribute to the understanding or treatment of gastric ulcer, although of course in any one case it may be found that there is a psychotic illness under everything.

There is one thing that must always be remembered, however, about psycho-somatic disorder, and that is that the physical part of the illness drags the psychological illness back to the body. This is of particular importance as a defence against a flight into the purely intellectual, that is to say a loss of psyche–soma significance in the individual. In this way the very early phenomena that have been described under the term primitive may become important in the study of any case with psycho-somatic disorder, gastric ulcer included.

It will be noted that a study of the current external factor can give results with statistical significance but can be extremely misleading.

APPENDIX

B. The Stage of Concern.

The Depressive Position (Klein) in Emotional Development.

The Theme of the Inner World.

The Withdrawn State: relation to (Preoccupation

(Concentration

The Paranoid State and Hypochondriacal Anxiety.

Four Types of Psycho-therapy material:

1. External relationships; imaginative elaboration.

2. Inner world inter-relationships.

3. Intellectual ramifications.

4. Transitional Phenomena.

Consideration of psycho-therapy setting

of quiet-excited states

of primitive and pre-primitive needs.

C. Primitive Emotional Development.

(a) Establishment of a relationship with external (shared) reality.

The theoretical first feed.

The value of illusion & transitional states.

The false self: normal & abnormal aspects

the caretaker self

the persona (cf. Jung).

(b) Integration. The attainment of unit status.

(c) Dwelling of psyche in body.

(d) The earliest states:

The earliest diagram: The Environmental–Individual Set-up.

The Birth Experience.

A primary state of being.

Chaos-order arising out of void.

III.

Evolution of Environment.

Study of Sequences (1) Imaginative elaboration of function.

Fantasy.

Inner reality.

(2) Inner reality;
Dream;
Fantasy;
Fantasying;
} Memory; creative art; play; work.

Development of Theme of Psycho-somatic Paediatrics.

Relationship to (1) normal functioning;
(2) neurosis;
(3) affective disorders;
(4) psychosis.

Transitional objects and phenomena.

IV.

Antisocial behaviour.

Delinquency related to environmental failure.

The Deprived Child.

V.

Latency.

Pre-puberty.

Adolescence.

Maturity.

SYNOPSIS II   *c.1967*

Various Types of Psycho-therapy Material.

Hypochondriacal Anxiety.

PART III.

The Ego Theory.   The Relationship to External
                         Reality: Play
                                              Creativity
                         Integration
                         Indwelling

                         Environment

BIBLIOGRAPHY

All books are published in London unless otherwise indicated.

Abraham, K. (1924) "A Short Study of the Development of the Libido, Viewed in the Light of Mental Disorders", in *Selected Papers on Psycho-Analysis*. Hogarth, 1927.

Aichhorn, A. (1925) *Wayward Youth*. Imago, 1951.

Balint, A. (1931) *The Psycho-Analysis of the Nursery*. Routledge & Kegan Paul, 1953.

Freud, A. (1926–27) *The Psycho-Analytic Treatment of Children*. Imago, 1946.

—— (1936) *The Ego and the Mechanisms of Defence*. Hogarth, 1937.

Freud, S. (1900) *The Interpretation of Dreams*, in James Strachey, ed. *The Standard Edition of the Complete Psychological Works of Sigmund Freud*, 24 vols. Hogarth, 1953–73 vols 4, 5.

—— (1905) *Three Essays on the Theory of Sexuality*, *S.E.* 7.

—— (1917) *Mourning and Melancholia*, *S.E.* 14.

—— (1923) *The Ego and the Id*, *S.E.* 19.

—— (1926) *Inhibitions, Symptoms and Anxiety*, *S.E.* 20.

—— (1931) *Female Sexuality*, *S.E.* 21.

Glover, E. (1932) *On the Early Development of the Mind*. Imago, 1956.

Gorer, G. and Rickman, J. (1949) *The People of Great Russia: A Psychological Study*. Cresset.

Guthrie, L.G. (1907) *Functional Nervous Disorders in Childhood*. Oxford University Medical Publications.

Henderson, D.K. and Gillespie, R.D. (1940) *A Textbook of Psychiatry for Students and Practitioners*, 5th edition. Oxford University Medical Publications.

Jackson, L. (1954) *Aggression and Its Interpretation*. Methuen.

Jones, E. (1927) "The Early Development of Female Sexuality", in *Papers on Psycho-Analysis*, 5th edition. Baillière, Tindall & Cox, 1948.

Klein, M. (1932) *The Psycho-Analysis of Children*, in *Collected Works*, vol. II. Hogarth, 1975.

—— (1934) "A Contribution to the Psychogenesis of Manic-Depressive States", in *Collected Works*, vol. I.

Middlemore, M. (1941) *The Nursing Couple*. Hamish Hamilton, 1941.

Money-Kyrle, R.E. (1951) *Psycho-Analysis and Politics: A Contribution to the Psychology of Politics and Morals*. Duckworth, 1951.

Ophuijsen, J.H.W. van (1920) "On the Origin of the Feeling of Persecution", in *Int. J. Psycho-Anal.* I.

Rivière, J. (ed.) (1952) *Developments in Psycho-Analysis*. Hogarth, 1952.

Rosen, J. (1953) *Direct Analysis: Selected Papers*. New York: Grune & Stratton, 1953.

Spence, J. (1946) "The Care of Children in Hospitals", in *The Purpose and Practice of Medicine*. Oxford University Press, 1960.

Spitz, R.A. (1945) "Hospitalism: An Inquiry into the Genesis of Psychiatric Conditions in Early Childhood", in *Psycho-Analytic Study of the Child*, I.

Winnicott, D.W. (1945) "Primitive Emotional Development", in *Through Paediatrics to Psycho-Analysis*. Hogarth, 1975.

—— (1949) "Mind and its Relation to the Psyche–Soma", in *Through Paediatrics to Psycho-Analysis*. Hogarth, 1975.

—— (1949) "Weaning", in *The Child, the Family and the Outside World*. Harmondsworth: Penguin, 1964.

—— (1950) "Some Thoughts on the Meaning of the Word 'Democracy'" in *Home Is Where We Start From*. Harmondsworth: Penguin, 1986.

—— (1968) "The Use of an Object and Relating Through Identifications", in *Playing and Reality*. Harmondsworth: Penguin, 1980.

INDEX